4-7-1901

To Esther. A

Carl

The Roads Taken:

A Country Lawyer Looks Back

by Kermit R. Mason

Edited by Carl B. Taylor, Ph.D.
and Kimberly J. Perry

mpc

McClain Printing Company
Parsons, West Virginia

1985

International Standard Book Number 0-9605948-2-5
Library of Congress Catalog Card Number 85-71615
Printed in the United States of America
Copyright © 1985 by Kermit R. Mason
Morgantown, West Virginia
All Rights Reserved

Dedicated to my mother, Winnie Welch Mason who was most responsible for my education; to my father, Raymond Walter Mason; to my wife, Rebecca Lashley Mason; to my sons, Thomas R., William L., and George R.; to my only daughter, Rebecca Mason Perry; to those who served in the military; to my fellow members of the legal profession; and lastly to my friend and neighbor, Carl Taylor, without whose encouragement and aid this book would never have been published.

THE ROAD NOT TAKEN

Two roads diverged in a yellow wood,
And sorry I could not travel both
And be one traveler, long I stood
And looked down one as far as I could
To where it bent in the undergrowth;

Then took the other, as just as fair,
And having perhaps the better claim,
Because it was grassy and wanted wear;
Though as for that the passing there
Had worn them really about the same,

And both that morning equally lay
In leaves no step had trodden black.
Oh, I kept the first for another day!
Yet knowing how way leads on to way,
I doubted if I should ever come back.

I shall be telling this with a sigh
Somewhere ages and ages hence:
Two roads diverged in a wood, and I—
I took the one less traveled by,
And that has made all the difference.

                                        Robert Frost

Contents

BOOK TWO—The Law Years

BOOK THREE—The Political Years

BOOK FOUR—Miscellaneous Personal Recollections

Introduction

Having begun my study of history in the days when this subject consisted mainly of a chronology of those events—principally political and military—which the authors of textbooks deemed worthy of memorization, I must confess that I found it neither especially interesting nor enlightening as a device for understanding the nature of our society. The individuals singled out for attention were mainly the national and tribal heroes—and villains. Little was to be found that gave us insights into the social and economic circumstances of the lives of the rank and file people once we passed beyond the sparse population of the American Colonies.

Local history is only one of the evidences of a change in approach. Surely some of the recent interest in it can be attributed to the manner in which it bridges the gaps between the lives of immediate ancestors and their descendants, between older and younger generations. Although some of the material resides in recorded sources, significant and often the more interesting aspects of historical experiences reside only in the storehouses of memories which older persons alone possess. All too often these become lost forever because they are not preserved by either those who possess them or by those to whom they are related in everyday conversations.

The present book is an exception to this because the author took the time to write down some of the more significant vignettes of those aspects of his own lifetime experiences covering eighty years plus. Some of the foundations on which these were built go back a couple of generations more. Here is history as it was lived and experienced by the writer.

Although the emphasis is primarily biographical, considerable attention is paid to the broader circumstances and the social setting from which the experiences emerged—in early rural Preston County and mid-century Monongalia County, West Virginia; and in the central European countries devastated by World War II. These aspects, together with the persistent search for the meaning and rationale of the experiences, give the contents as a whole a breadth which goes well beyond the personalized materials; hence there is also something of interest and importance in this book for those other than descendants, close friends, and associates.

Those people who have based their perception of Kermit Mason on only the public aspects of his life as an aggressive attorney, a hardheaded businessman, and a conservative, partisan politician with a naturally-endowed fiery temperament will see a much different side of his personality revealed. This shows through in his deeply-sentimental attachments to his family members; his concern for the powerless who were exploited and abused, whether by the economic system, the military hierarchy, or the governmental bureaucracy; his anger at injustice and inhumane treatment of people wherever it occurred; and his support for those who endeavored to improve the lot of their fellowman regardless of their status in life and their political affiliation.

Carl B. Taylor
Co-Editor, Neighbor, and Friend

viii

BOOK ONE

The War Years

A Soldier's Thoughts:
To My Three Sons and
My Two Ladies at Home

Fall of 1944—Italy

My earliest recollection of sound, it seems, even apart from my mother's lullaby, "Rock-a-bye baby in the tree top," was the patter of rain on a tin roof. Rain is pattering now, but it has a different sound, and it is in a different country. The sound I first remember was a pleasant, soothing sound; a sound to quiet the tired nerves. It seemed to say: "sleep, sleep, little one, in your protected world; you are safe, you will be cared for." The sound I now hear is the patter of rain upon a canvas tent in the mountains of Italy near a town called Anzio, a town where many have already died in a war, and where many more will die. This seems like a strange dream to me—or am I alive? Maybe I too, like my comrades, am already dead. How did I get here? Why did I come? Was this what I was born for? Was this why I so carefully planned my life? What am I to die for? I can't sleep for the noise of the guns. I lie awake and think. My life passes in review through my mind.

I was born in a little country village in West Virginia—a village snuggled away between two high mountains. A river flowed close by our house. I knew I could never cross the high mountains, but in my secret thoughts I knew that someday I would build a staunch, sturdy boat and drift down the river into a strange world where I would find fame and fortune. The house was huge, it seemed to me. It had been built by my grandfather after he had come home from the glory of the 'War Between the States.' He must have been foresighted, because he had planned it well. With eight rooms and a cellar, it was spacious for his family's needs. He planted trees, too; pine, maple, and locust for the east side; apple, peach, and cherry for the west. My grandfather and grandmother lived in this house when my mother married, and mother and father moved in to share the home. The house seemed to grow as we children came

3

into being. A new addition must have been added for each of us. There were three of us, and there were three additions to the house.

I had a dog—my first great earthly possession. His name was Rover—a funny-looking creature, black as coal. I loved him. The day he was kicked by a horse and his leg broken, I thought the world was ruined. But old Grammy, with her practiced hand, set his leg, and although he always ran on three legs thereafter, he was almost as good as new. Grammy, Bum Bum to most, once set the leg of a robin that some boy had broken with a thrown stone, and after it had healed the robin flew away. Then one day my heart was truly broken, because Rover died. Time, being good, healed the wounded heart, and I got another dog. He too died; but by then I'd grown to about six, and had learned that life could be hard.

I was just about six when I started to school. The teacher lived at our house, and she said she'd take care of me. I remember spending that year beside a big, fat Burnside stove in the middle of a room filled with desks. The teacher sat on a platform in front of a blackboard that stretched all the way across the room. The older boys said there was a trap-door under the teacher's desk, and that she put bad boys into the cellar. I believed this for a while, but later found out it wasn't true. About this time I'd begun to learn not to believe everything I heard. The Spring of my first year in school we boys got logs from the riverbanks and built a fort. We played war. Sometimes it was war with the Indians; sometimes, with the British. I didn't hate the British so then, as I hadn't begun to study early American history. When I got to the fourth grade, though, and began to study history, I really began to hate the British, because our histories had taught us they had treated us very meanly when we refused to buy their tea, and they had fought us because we wanted independence. Our histories didn't tell us we were part of Britain and had revolted. Yes, our histories had made us hate the British. They made us hate the Germans too, because they had fought against us on the side of the British for money. I resolved that some day I'd be a soldier, maybe a great general, and kill all the British and all the Germans.

There were two churches in my little village. Almost every-

4

body went to both. Sundays were gala days. All dressed in their best and went to Sunday School. Sometimes we children got to stay for church. It seems to me now that all my early childhood was built up around those two churches and the village school. My mother had been a country schoolteacher before her marriage. She had attended the county academy. She possessed about all the good books in the village, which probably, with the exception of the Bible, didn't exceed ten. *Ben Hur* was our favorite, and many an evening we spent during the winter around the fire, listening to her read.

Tonight when I hear the rain between the boom of the guns as it patters on my tent, I can close my eyes and see her there; the kerosene lamp with its polished globe radiating upon the pages of the book; we three children cuddled close by the fire, with father in the rocking chair; and mother reading until sleep came upon us and we were carried away to bed.

Father ran a country store. There, in the evenings, the sages gathered and discussed the affairs of the nation; yes, even of the world. Sometimes a book that was given to me for Christmas, *Lives of Famous Indian Chiefs,* was read. I realize now that Dad and the rest enjoyed the stories as I did. They, too, were being children again.

The years passed, one about the same as the other, with berry picking, swimming and playing in the summer; school in the winter—home with the family every night, Dad and Mother, Security, America—the Flag that was sacred. How strong we grew in its belief. How we loved the Stars and Stripes. Then came the "war to end wars"—1918. Peace, they said, shall exist in your time. I believed them. High school and college—what a grand day when I received the paper written in Latin that I still can't read, which made me a lawyer. I would make the world better. I would champion the rights of the oppressed. I would rout out the crooked politicians.

To my children

I married your mother; sweet, young, and good. You all came along; the years were happy. We built a mountain camp.

Each summer we added to it. There was a dog called Hector . . . a pony called Spot . . . remember? Then war clouds loomed, and war came. I said, "Take me, here I am." Your mother was silent. She didn't want me to go, but she said, "You won't be happy unless you go." And here I am tonight. Two years have gone by. Two years I've missed you, Tom, Dick, Bill, and Becky, big and little. Two years I've tried to serve my country, so that for you a better world may exist. Oh, yes, I've seen the blue waters of the Mediterranean, stood at midnight on the deck of a Liberty ship which was part of a giant convoy during a storm in the Atlantic. I've seen the grandeur of Africa, the pomp of Rome, the arts of the Egyptians and Italians, the dust of destroyed cities, ancient and new. But what I want now is a chance to see peace and happiness for you and the millions like you in this world.

I don't want you to be taught to hate. I want you to be taught to be just. I want you to be taught that America must be strong. Strong, not for war, but strong enough in war that she can preserve peace. You boys must stand for good, clean government, and a strong army built upon a system of merit and right. America will only survive if her people are willing to fight to prevent war. You must be educated. You, too, must wear the uniform of your country, but God forbid that you ever have to wear it in war!

Dawn is breaking. The candle is burning low—my writing must cease for there's work ahead. Come dawn some morning soon, and this nightmare ceases, I'll be coming back to you, to a new world, built upon peace, hope, and faith . . . but peace with the sword in one hand and the Bible in the other! It must be a world where all can have enough to eat, enough to wear. There must not be a chance for men like Hitler to get control of the people. But how, they ask, can we prevent it? Only by being honest and clean within America. Honest about our histories. I know now our histories lied about the British. I know it because I know them. I have many British friends, and they are our people—we come from British stock. They are our allies. They gave us our principles of liberty. We look alike, think alike.

We can do it by seeing how the Europeans and others live.

We can do it by ceasing to place all value upon a dollar basis. We can do it by a just and fair peace to those we conquer. We must learn such in our schools and in our homes. We must get understanding. We can only have understanding if we get the truth. Lonesome as I am here in my tent for the old tin roof in West Virginia, I am glad I had the courage to do what I thought was right, and you, my daughter, and my sons, must have the courage to act and think what is necessary to protect and preserve America.

The rain is ceasing, war continues. But even the years that seem long now will be short when peace comes.

> Maj. Kermit R. Mason, 0919903
> J. A. Sec. Hdq. Natousa
> Fall of '44
> Somewhere in Italy

November 1981
Morgantown, West Virginia

Almost 40 years ago I was walking in the woods with my daughter Becky, on a Sunday in the West Virginia hills. The date was December 7, 1941. We returned to our automobile to go home from the Cheat River mountains where we had been taking our walk. I turned on the car radio and much to my amazement I heard excited news reports saying that Pearl Harbor had been bombed and that now we were at war with the Japanese. "Becky, darling," I said, "your Daddy will have to join the Army and help defend his Country." The next day I wrote a letter to the War Department offering my services. Many months later, and only after I had an operation to correct a physical difficulty, I was commissioned a Captain in the U.S. Army. I reported for duty in Washington, D.C., in the Pentagon Building. A few months later, I was sent to the Judge Advocate School in Ann Arbor, Michigan. There I was taught military law for ten weeks and then assigned to the Eighth Service Command of the Army in Dallas, Texas. Having spent a couple of months in Dallas I was ordered to Fort Sam Houston, Texas, where I became the Post Judge Advocate and, as such, had charge of all legal matters in that command.

Fort Sam Houston was a very large army post. It consisted of about seventy-five thousand acres of land, which could almost be called an island within the state of Texas, in that only the federal government had jurisdiction over the same. Being the legal advisor to the Commanding General and a member of his staff, I rated a house on the post where, a few weeks later, my family joined me. During my stationing there, General Crammer visited us at Fort Sam Houston, and the Commanding Officer of the Fort assigned me to show him around and entertain him. Major General Crammer, a graduate of West Point, was the top legal lawyer for the U.S. ground forces in 1943. He was a Major General with headquarters in what was then the Munitions Building in D.C. and had been in the army during World War I. One of the places we visited was nearby Randolph Field, where General Crammer's old comrade and friend, General Airman, was the Commanding Officer. He was a Major General in the Air Force, and he, too, was a product of West Point and World War I.

At dinner that evening, the two generals reminisced about their past service and experiences in the armed forces. The following conversation I remember:

General Crammer to General Airman: "How are the boys coming along as soldiers in the Air Force?"

General Airman: "They are a fine lot! You know, I was afraid when the war started they would be a bunch of sissies and softies, but no! They are a finer group than we were during World War I. Of course, they like their fun and are reckless like we were. Why, do you know General Crammer, when I was a boy up in Missouri, I did a lot of reckless things too. It was only by the grace of God and some influential friends of my parents that a boyhood friend of mine and I didn't go to the penitentiary for stealing chickens. We were having a picnic and, just for the hell of it, stole some chickens from a neighbor's hen house. Now, my friend is president of the biggest bank in Denver, Colorado. The other day I was up in Denver and I phoned him. After about a half an hour, I finally got through his secretaries to him.

"Why you old chicken thief," I said, "How did you ever get to be the President of the biggest bank in Denver?" And then he said to me, "Why you damned old chicken thief, how did you ever get to be a two-star General in the U.S. Air Force?"

"Yes, General Crammer, I think our boys are O.K. They are great soldiers."

My family and I spent a very happy six months at Fort Sam Houston; however, believing the war was nearing an end, I wanted to get foreign duty and requested the same. I soon got it. I was a very happy officer New Year's night, 1943, when the telephone rang and Colonel Julian Hyer said, "Captain Mason, you are going overseas. Ready?" I said, "When?" He replied, "Soon." In a few days I was on my way to the port of embarkation. I stopped in Washington and learned that my destination was North Africa. I had left my good wife, Rebecca, my three sons, Thomas, William, and George, and my lovely daughter, Becky, at Fort Sam Houston. Returning home, I visited my mother in Morgantown, West Virginia. It was the last time I was to see her, for she died while I was in Italy, about a year later.

K. R. Mason, Major
0919903 J.A. Sec. Hdq.
SOS Natousa
APO 750
c/o Postmaster,
New York City

1944, Italy

10 August 1944

Dearest Becky,

The cable was a great shock. I'd hoped Granny would live until I came "around the corner" again, though when I said goodbye in January I felt it was for the last time. About the last thing she said was, "I wish I was 40 years younger, I'd be going myself."

This is Thursday. If the cable was not delayed, today was her funeral, about now. I left the office this AM and had a good cry, and a talk with the chaplain. I'm back now, as war stops not for death, and I feel better trying to be busy.

I feel she had a grand, happy life. I never knowingly did anything to hurt her. Upon the contrary, I felt deeply for what she had done for me and Gen and Medora, and tried hard to make some of it up to her.

There never was a woman who loved her kids more, and tried to give them a happy place in life. She possessed a courage beyond anything I've ever known. She was fearless, courageous, and loyal in everything she tried. I don't believe she had a selfish thought in her whole body. She loved you, darling, and you did more for her than anything I could have done. She was sublimely happy when you and I married, and as the kids came along, she idolized each and all of them.

She gave me a love of country, home, and family—a heritage to be proud of. Honor and pride were her virtues. She had her faults, but her virtues so overcame them that all her friends loved her. I'm sure she was happy, and I'm sure she is happy with Dad and Bum Bum now. Even here in far off Italy, I feel her presence. Death is the natural course of nature, and while she would have liked to have lived longer, I'm glad she passed away peacefully. I think "Come, grow old along with me, the best is yet to be . . ." fitted her life.

Honey, I need you right now, but I have the solace that I have you and your love. You are to me all she was . . . you have her virtues, and I'm proud she gave me the ideals that caused me to love you. Tommy, you filled my place with her. She loved you, and all the rest of the Mason kids. You were a man to her and I'm mighty proud of you . . . you are lucky to have had her for so long. You, my beautiful pumpkin, Becky . . . she will never be dead while you live, and I know you will grow up to be a fine lady like she was. You, Dick, she loved your noise and laughter; you helped her to wile away many an hour that would have been lonesome. You, wise old Bill, you read to her when you were five . . . you gave her much. I'm happy to have given her four such grandchildren.

Medora and Gen more than did their part. I want them to have what they want. She wrote a little will. It's among my insurance papers. Read it and keep it. Don't record it. It's her wish. I don't know what's in it, and regardless of it, Medora and Gen can take what they want. The house—don't rent it yet. Keep it as it is, if you want to, until I come home. Medora can use it if she wants to. Pay Charley Jenkins some and tell him I'll square the bill when I come home.

Honey, I know what you have been thru, and I'll try and make up for it when we all get together again. I hope and pray it won't be long. Don't feel sorry for Granny or me. I'm lucky to have had such a Mother. I could quote Lincoln, but you know it, so, because of her, and also because of you, darling, I've been a lucky man. She was a lucky woman. I'm glad I had the courage to do the things she would have done, and I'm glad you gave me part of that courage.

I love you, my darling, and will always continue to . . . for the kindness and fortitude you have shown her. I'll always love you for everything else you have given me.

I'll keep my chin up, looking for stars, and my hopes high, and some day ere long, we will all be together, laughing about the funny things Granny did, and the happy life she helped to give us all.

Until then, God bless and keep you all,
Yours forever,
Kermit

On to Oran, North Africa, 1942

I had thought my family would stay at Fort Sam until the children completed their school year since the oldest was only twelve; however, the country being at war, they were soon told to vacate our lovely post home, and they returned east to Morgantown, West Virginia. My orders of foreign duty took me first to Camp Patrick Henry, Virginia. It was a dismal place in swampy Virginia. We were quartered in an old wooden barracks that had been constructed during World War I. There we waited for our transportation for almost three weeks. I say we, for there I found twelve other Judge Advocate officers who were also going overseas. Finally the day arrived, and we boarded a train that took us to Hampton Roads Port, Virginia. We left the train and were marched down the wharf to a Liberty ship that was being loaded with huge bombs. I remarked to a friend, "Gee, I'd hate to have to cross the ocean on that!" Just then we were ordered to board that same ship, and up the plank we marched and down into the hold. The name of the ship was the *Felix Grundy*. The rear hold was filled with large bombs, and the forward hold contained six hundred fifty colored soldiers and us thirteen Judge Advocate Officers. Our quarters was the mental ward of the ship, which was the space usually allotted for six people.

Darkness came, the ship hoisted anchor, and we were soon under way. I don't think any of us slept much that night in our mental ward, nor did the 650 soldiers in the forward hold. When daylight came and the ship stopped, I went on deck. It was a sunny morning in February. The sight that greeted my eyes was amazing. There before me were almost a hundred ships: small airplane carriers, escort destroyers, one or two battleships and dozens of Liberty ships similar to the one I was on. Soon we were on our way clearing Hampton Roads and out into the broad Atlantic. We learned that the speed of our convoy was to be eight knots an hour, which was the speed of the slowest ship, and therefore, we who knew our destination knew we would be on the ocean for many days.

Liberty ships are very small and the problem of feeding and caring for close to 700 people, including soldiers and crew, was quite a job. The poor soldiers were confined most of the time to their cramped quarters in the hold. They played cards, sang and tried to pass the time as best they could. One of our men, Neil Hays, was appointed Chaplain for them, and he held many religious services whenever they requested such, which was frequently. About midway across the Atlantic the weather became very bad. The ocean waves ran very high. The ship tossed about, and many became very seasick. Those that did not become seasick were nauseated from the odor of those who had the sickness. The storm lasted for three or four days, and then the weather became calm again. On the deck in calm days, it was a marvelous sight to watch the other ships in our convoy plodding their way across the ocean. One could see the escort destroyers darting around our ships, forward, ahead, then behind the convoy, looking for the German submarine packs.

On the morning of the 20th day at sea, we started into the Strait of Gibraltar. I was on deck before daylight, and could see what was called the Europa light many miles ahead. When we entered the narrow Strait, I was surprised to see the bright lights of Spain on our left and darkened-out Africa on our right. Proceeding into the Mediterranean, we journeyed close to the African coast. The second day in this sea, German submarines attempted to attack us, but were driven off after considerable shooting had taken place. On the twenty-second day we entered the harbor of Oran, North Africa. A French pilot had boarded our ship before entering the harbor and accidentally piloted us into a sunken ship near the dock. I heard our Captain swearing and saying, "God damn you! I brought this ship three thousand miles through mine-infested waters and submarine packs, and now you ground it within a hundred feet of the dock!" We were mighty tired of the evil-smelling *Felix Grundy,* but still being a short distance from the dock we had to remain aboard for one more night until another ship was brought adjacent to us and the dock. By walking across it as a kind of footbridge, we made the shore of North Africa.

Oran, North Africa, was an amazing sight to us, particularly after 23 days shipboard. The harbor had many sunken ships from the North African invasion. Evidence was everywhere that the Germans had not welcomed us with open arms. We were soon placed in army trucks and journeyed some ten or twelve miles to a replacement depot, high on a hill overlooking Oran and the blue Mediterranean Sea. It was a bustling little city, filled with hundreds of soldiers awaiting assignment to various outlets. There we thirteen legal JA officers remained for some two weeks. Then we boarded a train, journeying to the beautiful city of Algiers where we reported for duty to the Judge Advocate's headquarters in the American Consulate Building.

[A Judge Advocate is simply an Army lawyer. His duties, among others, were to advise the staff to which he was assigned as to the military law, the rules of international warfare as adopted by the Geneva Convention, and to also act as legal advisor to the enlisted men, protecting their rights as soldiers against any abuses by the military authorities.]

Some of us were assigned to review court-martialed cases that had taken place earlier in North Africa while the others were shipped to their various assignments. I thought for a few days I was going to be sent to Anzio where there was very hard fighting. I was glad to remain for some weeks in Algiers doing legal work in that office before being ordered back to Oran. There on a high hill I reported to a General Larkin who was head of the unit called Comzone, the mission of which was to supply the Seventh U.S. Army that was preparing to invade southern France. I was assigned a position as acting Judge Advocate of this southern line of communication.

The building we occupied was a large prefabricated structure called a Nissen hut. It also contained the Inspector-General section and the Chaplain section of the U.S. Army. I was given a sleeping room in an old French hotel which was also occupied by bugs that worked on me during my sleeping hours.

My immediate Commanding Officer was a Colonel Hysson, a graduate of West Point, about forty years old. His health was not good, and he appeared to be very nervous. I soon learned that he had been in Sicily, and while there he had fallen in love with a woman who was supposed to be an Italian princess whose husband spent most of his time away from home. Every few weeks he would travel back to Sicily to see his mistress.

He was not an easy man to work for. Although he had been trained at West Point as a fighting soldier, for some reason he had been transferred to a law school in Washington, D.C.; thus he was free from combat duties.

I suggested many things we should do, such as keeping records and making reports on the treatment of soldiers who were court-martialed or were awaiting courts-martial. This he was not interested in. In fact, he seemed to be little interested in anything except the Princess in Sicily.

More than once during my post in Oran and Italy, I just barely escaped landing in "hot water"! Among my other duties as staff Judge Advocate was the giving of legal opinions to the staff officers concerning legal matters. Most of this staff consisted of high-ranking officers, ranging from lieutenant colonels to major generals. A General Dillon was the Provost Marshal of this outfit. He was also a lawyer, but having entered the army before World War II had commenced, and with

14

the great increase in the armed services after Pearl Harbor, he had attained the rank of Brigadier General. He was my "nemesis." He required many legal opinions, and after I had given them to him in writing, he would phone, seemingly taking great delight in attempting to prove that my opinions were legally wrong.

I had developed a close friendship during this period with a civilian doctor, O'Brien by name, who was then a Captain in the armed forces. We usually roomed together in Africa and Italy. He often told me his worries about doing administrative work and was afraid that he would be unable to practice his profession when he returned to civilian life. I, too, told him my problems. The worst, by far, had become the General of the Provost Marshal's office. My friend was an excellent mimic. He would frequently call me, changing his voice to sound identical to General Dillon, and would say something like, "Major Mason, this is General Dillon, Provost Marshal. I have before me your legal opinion in the Private Smith affair, and am sorry to say I don't agree with you." Of course, there was not much to say to a Brigadier General in return since I was only a Major.

An especially embarrassing incident involving these two men occurred one time after we had moved to Italy. The long days were trying in the hot sun of July in southern Italy, and my good friend, Captain O'Brien, would frequently call me pretending he was General Dillon, really taking me apart. One hot afternoon the phone in my Judge Advocate office rang, and a voice said, "This is General Dillon, and Major Mason, I think you are wrong again in your opinion of Lt. Brown's case." I was sure it was my doctor friend Captain O'Brien, so I said, "Go to hell, you son of a bitch." The phone almost exploded, and then too late I realized it really was General Dillon. How I escaped a court-martial I'll never know; but believe me, General Dillon, no doubt to this day, believes his legal advisor had really become shell-shocked!

There seemed to be great temptations among the G.I.'s of WW II to fall in love with the young ladies of the countries in which we fighting the war and to want to marry them. For this reason, it was necessary to obtain permission to marry through the highest authority in each command section. Among those

15

required to review and approve the applications to marry was the Judge Advocate, who was required to look into the legal status of the applicants, and the theatre chaplain, who was required to look after the problems of religion and morals. One particular request came before me involving a 19-year old colored soldier from Louisiana, Private George Washington Faulkner. He had filed an application to marry a Belgium girl, a Miss Law, in a nearby village. After finding the applicants legally qualified to marry, I sent the application to my friend Padre Moran, the Catholic father who represented that respective faith in our staff, as the young lady was of the Catholic faith.

Padre Moran visited Youlinda in her home where the following conversation took place: "I am Father Moran of Comzone, a Major in the U.S. Army, and I want to talk to you about your desire to marry Private George W. Faulkner." "Yes, Father," responded Youlinda, "I want very much to marry George and live with him in America after this awful war is over." "You know Louisiana law," said Father Moran. "George is a colored man, and if you marry him and go back to the States you may run into some embarrassing situations since blacks and whites seldom marry there." "Oh, no," assured Youlinda, "George told me he was originally white, the same as all of us, but the Army had injected a chemical into his blood to make him black so he couldn't be seen at night. He said he belonged to a group of night fighters and, being black, couldn't easily be seen at night. After the war is over, he will be injected with a chemical that will make him white again. So you see Father, there wouldn't be any problem." I have often wondered what happened to this strange request to marry.

As amusing as some incidents may have been, I was still surrounded by grim reminders that war has many ugly and pathetic effects upon the men and women it encompasses. John Smyther, Jr., represented the small but ever present fraction of individuals unable to sanely handle war's nightmares. The Military Post Office (the APO) was on the edge of the city of Oran. It was a very small building and was staffed by three non-commissioned officers, two sergeants, and two corporals. John Smyther, Jr., was one of the corporals. He was twenty-four years old and possessed a Ph.D. in psychology from the

16

University of Southern California. He was a very lonely individual and talked very little to his fellow soldiers. On a spring morning in May, he shot and killed his three fellow employees, and then disappeared into the hills above Oran. Early the next morning a shot was heard near an anti-aircraft gun. When it was investigated, Corporal Smyther was found with a bullet in his temple and his carbine clutched in his hands. As the Staff Judge Advocate, I reviewed what the Army called a "line of duty report." It contained the young corporal's army diary, in which he complained of the boredom of army life. The final entry read, "I told the army psychologist in California when I was drafted into the army in 1942 that I could not take army life. Journey's end May 25, 1943."

Southern Italy, 1944

By July 1944, our mission in Africa had been completed. We journeyed to southern Italy to begin supplying the great U.S. Fifth Army and other troops that were fighting the Germans north of Naples. Anzio, Cassino, and Rome had not yet fallen, and were occupied and controlled by Hitler, along with his fellow henchmen under the disgusting leader of the Italian people, Mussolini.

Our headquarters was at Caserta, about twenty-five miles north of Naples on the old Appian Way, near the old King of Naples' palace. The palace was the Allied Headquarters, hence occupied by the British, French, and many other groups.

I frequently visited Naples, passing nearby the Mount Vesuvius volcano which was sometimes emitting smoke. One Sunday while visiting a friend there, from a nearby hill I saw and counted more than one thousand ships in the Naples harbor. These were a part of the Seventh Army that we had been equipping in Africa, which was now shipboard on their way to invade France. The remaining hundreds of other ships transporting this great army were in the harbor of Sardinia. I was always amazed at the vastness of our armies and what it took to transport them.

Conditions in Italy were then horrible for the civilians. You will recall that Italy tried to surrender, whereupon the Germans completely occupied that country, and it was necessary to fight them from town to town and house to house. The houses being made mostly of stone, they made excellent fortifications for the Germans. The Italian people were at the mercy of the Germans. The civilians were literally starving, their homes were being destroyed, and poor little children were crying for food.

My West Point Colonel managed to get himself transferred to Naples, and I was left in charge; but still being only a Captain then, it was necessary for me to sign all opinions, "Mason for Hysson." He would not only disagree with many of my legal opinions, but would even send some of them to the General without giving me a chance to make them conform to his legal thinking, of which I had a very low opinion.

Anzio, Cassino, and Rome all fell, and I visited them. I was surprised that any men lived through their battles. Vast areas were completely destroyed. The smell of dead bodies of fighting men, both enemy and friend, was everywhere. I crossed the Anzio battlefield and marveled how any of our soldiers survived since it was a flat plain, and the Germans were high on a hill with their weapons trained on our boys on the open flats below. Hundreds of our men were wounded and died there, in my opinion, needlessly.

Rome was largely spared, though our Air Force did bomb the railroad stations, killing many Italian civilians. I visited the ancient city and toured the beautiful Saint Peter's Cathedral. There were only two of us there that day, and a friendly Italian guide took us up on the roof from which we looked into the Gardens of the Vatican.

The reader may no doubt recall that when the Italians killed some retreating Germans, more than three hundred Italians, men, women, and even children were murdered in the Catacombs. No mercy was shown. Hitler had well-trained his youths who believed they were the master race. The Romans were jubilant to see the American troops replace the cold-blooded Germans.

One of my assignments was to inspect a prisoner of war camp in the city of Livorno, a much-bombed and heavily destroyed city. Here, we temporarily housed the German soldiers who had surrendered to our troops until we could place them on Liberty ships which had discharged our army's cargo in the port, and then load them with prisoners to be transported to Prisoners of War Camps in the United States. They were usually put to work in the United States, and the problems of feeding and guarding them in the war zone were eliminated.

These camps in Italy were usually inspected by Swedish Red Cross people, and we did not want reports of bad treatment of prisoners of war to get back to the Germans who, in turn, would mistreat our soldiers who had surrendered to them.

I found the camp very muddy—a regular hog pen—and recommended that the Germans be moved as soon as possible. In fact, the prisoners were almost covered by mud as the camp was in low land and more rain than usual had fallen.

Later I was ordered on a mission that took me to our Italian front line. High in the Apennine Mountains, more than one hundred miles north of Florence, was the front line at a place called Castle del Rio. From there one could look into the Po River valley not far from the city of Bologna. This was my first time under shell fire, and I must say it not only made me a very humble person, but also more considerate of the soldier who sometimes refused to obey orders to advance under fire. Bodies of dead Germans awaiting burial were lying around, and many prisoners were being escorted to the rear of the line. On our way back to Florence at night, we traveled through many searchlights that were being used to prevent the Germans from making surprise attacks in the darkness. Florence had been spared heavy shelling and still remained a beautiful city on the Arno.

On this trip I saw many of our fine soldiers in the mist, cold rain and snow of the Apennines where they had been for many months, fighting the Germans. The entire Italian war was one of horror and dismay. The Italian people did not want war. Their leader had gotten them into it. When they wanted to quit, the Germans invaded their country and made every village a stone fortress as they fought the Americans and British. The civilians suffered terribly—hunger, cold, and in many

19

instances death were their lot. I can never forget the pale children and women standing beside the roads, begging for something to eat as we traveled the war-torn roads of Italy.

The Italian war became a stalemate. I'm sure the Italian people wanted to surrender and end the war for more than a year before they found it possible to do so. The Germans just wouldn't let them quit. The fighting bogged down near the place I had visited, Castle del Rio, for almost the whole next year before Germany was about to surrender.

When I returned to our headquarters in Caserta, I had a phone call from Colonel Hysson telling me to go to Oran, Africa and inspect what was called a Rehabilitation Center— telling me also that when the European war was over much trouble would be encountered in sending our European troops to the Far East to fight Japan. I doubted this, and dreaded the flight of more than a thousand miles in an ancient C-47 plane. However, I obeyed orders and journeyed to Oran, the old city I had left some six months before. The next morning after arriving there, I journeyed to the Rehabilitation Center a few miles into the African desert.

The purpose of such a center is what the name implies. A soldier who had committed a military offense was first tried by a court-martial. If found guilty, as was always the case, the usual sentence was a term in prison, a dishonorable discharge, and a suspension of all pay and allowances; but in many cases the sentence was suspended, and he was sent to the Rehabilitation Center. If he made good there, in about six months the sentence was reconsidered, and he was returned to his outfit or a replacement unit for further duty.

There were more than a thousand soldiers confined in the Oran Center. Their usual day commenced at 5:00 A.M. and continued until way late at night. One of the scheduled activities each day was a twenty-five mile march in the hot African sun. No leaves were granted. The treatment of the soldiers seemed to me to be very brutal, but I was advised by those conducting the center that the objective was to treat them so harshly that they would soon be glad to be restored to active duty.

I obtained all the rules and information available and left the following morning at 3:30 A.M. for Naples. When daylight came, we were flying very close to the Atlas Mountains. The plane was loaded with barrels. As we proceeded, the trip encountered rough air, and it was necessary for us to attempt to tie them down. The only other passenger on the plane with me was a new arrival, a young lieutenant in the navy. You, no doubt, know which of us was more frightened on that trip, he or I. I know he became very pale, and I sweat more than usual.

Upon my return I delivered all the information to Colonel Hysson; but I am sure he never even looked at my report.

The Case of John and Mary—and the Priest That the General of the U.S. Army Wanted to Court Martial

Man has an unerring sense of survival, even in the hardest of times. Life went on, the sun rose, and a few managed to turn their eyes away from war's pessimism. In the desolation that befell the Italian front, the needless killing was not the only example of insensitivity and blind pride.

Once again I was confronted with what the army had deemed a questionable matrimonial circumstance. John Smith, a major in the U.S. Air Force, and Mary Brown, a U.S. Army nurse, were both stationed on the island of Sardinia in 1943. They were both from Texas, although they had never met until a USO dance. They fell in love, and both being single applied through their command channels for permission to marry. Many weeks went by, and, although they made frequent inquiries, nothing was heard of their request to marry. The Commanding General apparently did not favor members of his command getting married.

John and Mary were members of the Catholic faith, so they consulted Father Thomas Jones and requested that he marry them. Father Jones was a Chaplain and a Captain in the U.S. Air Force. He told them he was without authority to marry them without the consent of the Commanding General. The couple pleaded with the Chaplain to just go through the marriage ceremony of their faith, requesting simply the formal

21

ceremony which would be the blessing of the Church. They must have looked sympathetic as the good Father did as they requested. He did not report them as married. John and Mary soon commenced living together and told their friends that they were husband and wife. When the Commanding General of the U.S. Army in Sardinia heard of their marriage, he ordered them all court-martialed, including the good priest, Father Jones! The case came to my office for legal disposition. Having been a country lawyer for many years before entering the military service, I knew I was handling a very touchy legal matter and a matter of public relations that could become very embarrassing for the military authorities, including my two-star major general. I had few legal books from which to research the laws of marriage and the many legal problems involved. I did know the United States law favored marriage; but how was I to determine the violation of the army regulations forbidding marriages without the consent of the army authorities?

I finally wrote the following opinion which was approved by my General, and the matter legally ended: (1) The American law favored marriages, and in many States, including Texas where both John and Mary were residents, representation to the public by a man and woman that they were husband and wife, and living together as such, constituted what was known as common law marriage; and that having done such, John and Mary were now legally married and were husband and wife. Further, it would be a breach of public policy to punish them now; to do so would possibly create a scandal for the military authorities. The military could not dissolve the marriage since marriage was a legal contract between only two parties, and they had made such a contract. (2) The good priest had not violated the military law. He told John and Mary that he could not pronounce them husband and wife. He merely gave them the blessings of the Church. To court-martial a priest would be a great abuse of authority for a Commanding General of the U.S. Army to commit. Now I had them legally married, and apparently the generals had been properly worried, for my opinion was approved and the matter ended. I often wondered what happened to the legal common law marriage of John and Mary. I often felt that I had performed their marriage ceremony.

On to France, 1944

In September 1944 I was ordered to France since the Seventh Army had already invaded the southern part of that country. On a cloudy day I flew as a passenger in an army bucket-seated C-47 from the Naples Airport over the water by way of Sardinia, always on the lookout for the German planes that were close by. One fighter plane was spotted, but our pilot managed to get into a bank of clouds and prevent an attack. Traveling up the Rhone Valley, we soon landed safely in the beautiful old city of Dijon in central France. Our mission was to continue supplying the frontline troops, among them being General Patton's Third Army and General Patch's Seventh Army. My headquarters was at the Lycee Carno, a French Junior College.

We had military jurisdiction over a vast military complex called Base Sections: ports and railroads that delivered the vast stores of military equipment required to keep an army on the move in a large theatre of war. Our staff was large, consisting of many high-ranking officers. General Larkin, a Major General, was our Commanding Officer.

The Germans had tried, under Hitler's command, to break through the allied fronts in northern France and had failed. The battle for Germany was about to commence. There was an air of excitement at our headquarters in Dijon for the reason that General Brehon Somerall, the Commanding Officer of the Service of Supply for all the war zones, was coming out from Washington; and a staff meeting had been called for all the commanding generals of the fronts in France. Meetings were held. We were told to be ready to answer any questions that the General would ask. However, it was stated that no reports would be asked of the Staff Judge Advocate or the Chaplain. I rather doubted this because I knew that when General Somerall was in Italy he had demanded reports from the Staff Judge Advocate as to the treatment of enlisted men. I stated as much to my immediate superior, a Colonel in a section known as GI, to which he promptly told me in very firm tones that I was out of order. He reiterated that no report would be required from the Judge Advocate. Silently, I was unconvinced; for two of our important duties were (a) the requirement of maintaining records of the number of enlisted men who had been arrested for offenses and placed in stockades or military jails, and (b) the responsibility for seeing that the soldier's legal right to a speedy trial was protected.

The day arrived for the meeting. I had never seen General Somerall. The various staff officers were assembled. There were nineteen generals, many colonels, and numerous other high-ranking officers assembled in their finest uniforms with decorations, when a very large, tall, fine-looking soldier strolled into the room. He was dressed in the uniform of a field soldier. A brace of pistols in shoulder holsters were strapped to his shirt. He greeted the assembly. As a major, I was the lowest grade of all the officers present.

"Gentlemen," he said. "I was a young captain of engineers in this city of Dijon during World War I and God damned nearly got court-martialed for building a railroad across a hop field here!" "Now," he continued, "I want a report from the Adjutant as to how the mail from home is getting through to the soldiers." General Larkin called on his Adjutant, a young colonel, for the report. It was apparently highly unsatisfactory to General Somerall, for he stated to General Larkin, "You had better get a new adjutant. Morale suffers when men don't get their mail from home." He was very firm and adamant. He had two sergeants with him who seemed very skilled in shorthand as he was continuously dictating instant orders.

The next request from General Somerall to General Larkin was a report from the Staff Judge Advocate. I was it! I had been advised that no report would be required. The following conversation took place:

Colonel of G1: "Major Mason is our Staff Judge Advocate and will give you any desired information."

"I want to know," said General Somerall, "how many soldiers are confined in the Base sections under this command, and I want to know the time from confinement to trial, and the time from trial to final action."

I was ready for this very situation to arise, and replied, "390 men confined in Delta Base Section, average time from confinement to trial, 80 days. Time from trial to final action, 85 days."

24

There was a loud roar from General Somerall. "Larkin, what the God damn hell do you mean? Don't you know we send soldiers here to fight? Don't you know we don't send them here to lie around in stockades? Don't you know that men should be tried and their cases completely disposed of within 30 days?"

I knew this, and had been reporting the same to G1 for months. However, I thought I would try to protect my General and said, "Sir, many of the offenses for which these men are charged were committed in the States prior to troop movement overseas, and, thus, in some cases the long delay."

This did not improve the situation, and General Somerall immediately dictated an order requiring all soldiers to be immediately tried, their cases disposed of, or released, again saying in very firm tones, "We don't place soldiers in our Army to confine them in prison at the whims of some higher authorities. Carry out my orders in this respect or court-martial all your subordinates who do not do so!" I was greatly embarrassed, because, although making a factual report, I knew I had greatly humiliated my General.

Next, General Somerall said, "Now I want a report from the officer in charge of engineers."

A Brigadier General arose and said, "Sir, I am in charge of engineers."

"I want to know," said General Somerall, "how long it will take you to bridge the Rhine River with railroad bridges in order that we can get our trains across when the breakthrough comes?"

The Brigadier replied, "Six weeks, Sir."

General Somerall again erupted, "What's wrong with you? Julius Caesar bridged the Rhine in 13 days."

"Julius Caesar didn't have tanks," stammered the Brigadier.

"Any darn fool knows that," scoffed General Somerall. "How did you get that star on your shoulder?"

The meeting soon ended. The breakthrough came. I was soon transferred to a front line outfit, but I've always been glad I told General Somerall the truth.

25

The 'Battle of the Bulge'

The belief that all that remained of the European War was the final offensive thrust into Germany from a variety of directions was very pervasive during November and early December. The optimism even went so far occasionally for us to hear the words or tune of the song, "I'll Be Home for Christmas." A few officers were given long overdue leaves, including General Montgomery for a trip back to England. A counteroffensive by the Germans was almost inconceivable, but on December 16 Hitler, against the advice of his top generals, launched what was to become known as the "Battle of the Bulge." This final major thrust was a last desperate attempt to break through the Allied lines, surround some of the troops, re-capture the vitally important port of Antwerp, and drive the British army north into the sea. Preparations were made in the greatest secrecy.

It was indeed a sad sight to see hundreds of trucks carrying soldiers through Dijon on their way to the front around Christmas time. The weather was very cold, and it was snowing part of the time. Some of the soldiers were even singing, "I'm Dreaming of a White Christmas"—but many had already seen their last Christmas, and for huge numbers of others this was to be their last one.

During almost two weeks of this renewed thrust, the Allied planes were grounded by the dismally cold, foggy weather which was ideal for the travel of the German land forces as they moved through the Ardennes forest. The situation was very serious, and even we staff officers were suddenly armed. Perhaps an important reason for this developed out of a new, surprise tactic. Hitler had ordered SS Major Otto Skorzeny to form a unit of English-English and American-English speaking soldiers dressed in captured British and American uniforms, complete with identification tags. They were to break through the lines, seize bridges, demoralize the enemy, and perhaps even assassinate high-ranking officers. He found only a few who had the necessary language ability, but others were to accompany these and pretend that they were too frightened to talk. They killed many of our soldiers who first believed them to be their comrades. In retrospect, it has been concluded that this mission accomplished few of the major objectives; but, as Drew Middleton wrote forty years later, "A bad case of spy fever was provoked in the Allied rear areas."

Eventually the weather cleared, and one sunny morning we heard the roar of hundreds of planes. It was a wonderful sight to see our air forces heading in the direction of the "bulging" lines. This barrage continued for several days, and soon von Rundstedt's elite troops were running in the direction of home.

It has been said that more American soldiers were killed in the Battle of the Bulge than in all the Japanese Pacific War. It was the heaviest battle toll in American history; but Hitler's gamble had failed.

War is really hell! It seems that only the youth die in it while old men sit at home telling our government officials that the wars must continue!

The Case of Private Bill Smith

Among the hundreds of army regulations for the conduct of military affairs in 1944, during WW II, was one commonly referred to as Section VIII. This regulation provided for an honorable discharge from military service for those individuals for whom, for any reason, their Commanding Officer deemed best for the soldier as well as advantageous to the military service. The discharge simply read, "He is no longer suitable for military service." Private Joe Smith was a nineteen-year-old soldier, whose home was in the mountains of Kentucky. He had been the driver of Captain Brown's jeep for eighteen months commencing with maneuvers in Louisiana, and, finally, on the long push through northern France to the German border. Upon at least five occasions, under fire from the Germans, he had stopped the jeep and run to nearby road culverts, or into the adjacent woods. He had been warned time and again by Captain Brown that repetition of such behavior would lead to a serious court-martial.

The sixth time this incident occurred, Captain Brown filed general court-martial proceedings against Private Smith. The

27

private was greatly excited about the charge and feigned loss of his mental faculties. Upon advice of the battalion physician, Private Smith was given a Section VIII discharge and was returned to his home in Kentucky, instead of being court-martialed. Captain Brown sought my services as the Judge Advocate of the Twenty-first Corps. He handed me a letter written by Private Smith to one of his buddies in the Captain's company and said to me, "This man must be punished. He has wrecked the morale of my company, and I want him returned to the Army." I read the following letter from Private Smith to his buddy:

> Dear Pal Bren,
>   Here I ere in old Kentucky, a seeing my girl, huntin, drinkin and fishin. Ask Captain Brown who in the hell ere crazy now?!
>   Bill Smith

I was forced to advise the Captain that since Private Smith had been Sectioned VIII out of the army there was nothing more he could do. He was a very angry Captain when he left my office!

The Case of Yvette and the Court-Martials of Nelse and Sole

Of all the cases I handled as Judge Advocate during the Second World War, the case of Yvette leaves the greatest impression upon me—perhaps because it was the starkest example of injustice within the judicial system, particularly in the military.

"You, and each of you, are hereby sentenced to forfeit all pay and allowances, to be dishonorably discharged from the armed service, and to be hanged by the neck until dead." The place was somewhere in France near the German border on a day in April 1944. They were two American soldiers, ages nineteen and twenty. They had entered the American army from Massachusetts, one as a volunteer, and the other drafted in 1942. The sentence that had just been read to them was pronounced by a Colonel, a member of the five-member all-officer court. Nelse and Sole were escorted by their military police

28

guard to a French farm house—half house, half barn—which was to be their prison for a few days, until they were to be taken to a French jail. The American Lieutenant who had been appointed to defend Nelse and Sole had advised them not to testify in their trial, which was a charge of rape of a French girl. He assured them as they were being led away that their sentence would be reviewed by the Commanding General of the Seventh Army.

Colonel Brown, who had just read the sentence to Nelse and Sole, looked at his associates and said, "Now, gentlemen, this will please our French friends and scare the hell out of the other G.I.'s in France. Let's repair to the Officer's Club for a small libation." Prentice Price was the Public Relations Officer of the Seventh Army Headquarters, and his presence at the trial, together with that of the French Liaison Officer, had been requested by Colonel Brown, the Judge Advocate of the Seventh Army Headquarters. He was told to write a news release for the *Stars and Stripes,* the army newspaper, which he did as follows:

France, April 20, 1944.
   A U.S. Army Courts-Martial in France today sentenced Nelse and Sole, two soldiers of the U.S. Army, to be hanged for the rape of a French female. The sentence of death is expected to be approved by the Commanding General of the Seventh Army, and thereafter will be reviewed by the Commanding General of this theatre. Major Currie, French Liaison Officer, was present at the trial, and thereafter stated he believed the sentence would improve relations between the French civilians and American soldiers, and took steps to see that full publicity was given the sentencing of the soldiers in French newspapers.

For six long months Nelse and Sole languished in the military jail, expecting any day to be notified that the sentence of death would be carried out. Then they were advised that General Dwight D. Eisenhower had ordered the Commanding General of the Seventh Army to grant the soldiers a new trial since it did not appear that they had been given a fair trial by the army court that originally tried them. The six months awaiting the carrying out of the sentence of death showed its effects upon the soldiers since they were inexperienced young

29

boys in a game run by old men. My orders came the same day the order had been presented to Colonel Brown stating that the trial of Nelse and Sole was illegal. The effect upon the Colonel was disconcerting. He believed his General had been humiliated. He believed the soldiers should have been executed. This was bad for morale and discipline in the armed forces. Now there was a new trial, another Courts-Martial to be appointed, and another order with which to disturb his General. A staff conference was held in the legal department of the Seventh U.S. Army Headquarters in Luneville, France, and the suggestion was made, "Why not appoint the new Major who had just started his position in the Seventh Army? Had he not been on General Eisenhower's staff? This was a delicate case, involving life and death as well as public relations with our ally, France." I received my first order in the Seventh Army and thus became the defense counsel for Nelse and Sole.

Chaplain Moran was a Catholic Priest. He belonged to that missionary group of Paulists who believed their duty was to teach the religion of Christ by helping and aiding their fellowman. He had served in China, and was there when Pearl Harbor was bombed. He immediately came home to the State of Massachusetts and enlisted in the Chaplains' Corps of the U.S. Army. Now he was the Chaplain for the battalion to which Nelse and Sole were attached, and which was fighting the Germans near the German and French border, near Luneville, France. He knew Nelse and Sole; they were members of his parish. He had served their religious needs, and they had regularly attended his mass from North Africa where they had made the first assault on the beaches, to Anzio, where both soldiers had been decorated for bravery, and now the German border. Father Moran had not known of the arrest and conviction of Nelse and Sole until after their sentence of death had been pronounced. He was then very disturbed and agitated. He stormed into the Seventh Army Headquarters and demanded to see the General. This he was refused. He became very angry with the Judge Advocate, and demanded the death sentence be changed for the two soldiers. Then he violated army regulations and procedure by writing a letter directly to General Eisenhower. The General probably never saw the letter, but
30

somehow the results had nevertheless been obtained. The Priest was being threatened with trial, but two members of his organization were at least temporarily being saved from death.

I was briefed by the august Staff Judge Advocate of the Seventh U.S. Army: "You see, Mason, I am appointing you to defend these men. They both should have been hanged weeks ago. What they did to this little French girl was awful. The General felt so terrible about it, he even consulted with the French officers assigned to his staff."

I was told the French people were becoming greatly disturbed by the conduct of the American soldiers; that they even feared them more, in some instances, than the Germans. "You know, Mason, that we must get and keep the respect of the French. We must show them that we are good, respectable people. These soldiers must be executed. I know you have a responsibility as a defense attorney, but remember your duty to your country. We must have the respect of France. We must have law and order in our Army."

I replied, "Sir, if I am assigned to defend these men, I'll do my best to see that they have a fair trial." Thereupon, the conference ended, and from then on the relations between the Staff Judge Advocate of the Seventh Army and myself were not very cordial.

I was given the record of the first trial of Nelse and Sole by Lieutenant Smith who had defended them in their first trial. He was a timid second lieutenant. He advised me that Nelse and Sole were guilty as hell. He told me he always was interested in law, and hoped to study it someday. I asked, "Why didn't you place these soldiers on the witness stand and let them explain their side of the story?" He gave me no explanation but simply handed me the records of the first trial which contained only the testimony of Yvette, the accusing witness, the findings of the court, and the dishonorable discharge and death sentence of the soldiers. I asked for a desk and a stenographer in the legal section of the Seventh Army Headquarters, but I soon detected a coolness there which was more than the weather of northern France in Luneville in that month of February 1944. I was again the country lawyer, only now I was defending two young boys in France; boys who had been condemned to death and now given a reprieve, temporarily. I hoped for more, but I noted that there was an air of determination by someone to see that these boys died.

I located my clients in a French jail in Luneville—an old, ugly, cold stone prison, probably built the year Marie Antoinette was beheaded during the French Revolution. I introduced myself to Nelse and Sole and stated that I was now their new defense counsel. I was, as always, surprised at the youth of my clients; after more than two years in the U.S. Army I still could hardly believe our American soldiers were mostly clean-cut, fair-haired young boys that one should see back home in high school. Nelse was nineteen. He had been in the service two years. Sole was twenty, and had spent three years in the armed forces. They were pale, frightened, and nervous. They had ceased to be heroes, driving the enemy from a defeated nation. Now they were condemned to die, accused of assaulting a girl whom they had freed from the enemy in a country that had been unable to defend itself. Their first words to me, almost simultaneously, were, "We didn't rape her!" Now I knew I had a defense. There were two of them. There would be a chance. There would be a reasonable doubt.

I knew I would probably not win my case before a Courts-Martial appointed by the Seventh Army General. I knew the Courts-Martial procedure was similar to hand-picking your jury, where you also select the prosecutor. The prosecutor and sometimes the defense counsel are advised that it will be a great displeasure if the wishes of the appointing General are not carried out. I knew that I must, as lawyers say, build a record for these soldiers on paper in the form of a complete written history of them from the day that they came into the army until the day they were accused of the crime. This record was to be for the future. I knew they would be found guilty again by the new Courts-Martial. The saving of face of the staff and the general who had signed the first death sentence was involved in this case. This would be no ordinary trial. This was to be a test of me. Was I bold and daring enough to do my duty as defense counsel for the two young soldiers? I knew this record must be made from the time that they entered our army and now they were in a strange land, away from their home, family, and friends. There would be only their fellow soldiers and officers of their organization from whom to get information and testimony as to their character and reputation.

The Military of the U.S. Army is a self-contained organization. It does things by the rules; right or wrong exists when you depart from these rules. The military law of the U.S. Army in 1944 was all contained in a small book called "Manual of Courts-Martial." Therein was the set procedure which had been followed by the U.S. Armed Forces since the days of George Washington. Our military law system, we were told, followed, or was copied from, the early-day German army, as taught to us by German officers who aided us in the American Revolution. It had been changed but little in more than one hundred years. The Manual of Courts-Martial was so designed that a person not trained in the legal procedure of American courts could follow the "book" in the trial, and thereafter present a court record that contained few errors as to the right procedures. In fact, army court stenographers frequently used the forms and copied the same from the book, regardless of how the case was presented. Under the law, I had the right to demand separate trials for Nelse and Sole, and this I promptly did. This was granted. I asked for time and was given ten days to prepare my cases for trial.

In civilian life, when a person is charged with a serious crime involving death, many people arise to his aid. However, here two young men were in a strange land, thousands of miles from home and friends. Their parents, of course, were without knowledge of the charges. Their only friend that they knew, or that I knew, was Chaplain Moran. He was indeed a true friend and valiant warrior. He was fearless of both the high-ranking officers of the mighty Seventh U.S. Army, and also of the Germans who then were desperately fighting our troops a few miles away. He and I rode mile after mile over the war-torn roads, visiting the outfit to which Nelse and Sole belonged, then in combat. We talked to the Battalion Commander, the Company Commander, the Sergeant, Corporal, and many others who had been fighting side by side with Nelse and Sole for almost two years. Many of their friends, however, had been killed in the fighting from North Africa, Anzio, and the hedge-

33

rows of France, and were not now available to come to their aid. I learned from these officers and comrades of Nelse and Sole the lesson I was to observe over and over again in war; that there is an affinity or bond between men who constantly face death over and over again that consists of deep respect which these men have for one another. I was told again and again by officers and enlisted men of Nelse and Sole of acts of courage and valor previously performed by both of these soldiers, and how they fought and lived with their fellowmen. I now knew I could build a record of fighting American soldiers who were brave and courageous. Thus I prepared for trial.

The army law, as set forth in the previously described manual, seemed to me to be very harsh. Rape was punishable by death, or as a Courts-Martial may determine. I had seen many circulars written by our army as we journeyed from Africa to Italy, and then to France and Germany, advising the American soldiers that they were now in strange lands and that they would be exposed to many strange people and customs. I kept wondering what the punishment for a French youth in France would be if he had committed the same crime these soldiers were charged with having committed. I decided to consult a French lawyer who was then a Colonel in the French Army assigned to the Seventh Army Headquarters as a liaison officer.

The trial day arrived and the court assembled. It consisted of an Eagle Colonel, a Lieutenant Colonel, a Major, a Captain, and a First Lieutenant. The military law provides for a President of the Courts-Martial and a law member. The President acts as a Judge does when maintaining civilian courts, and is advised by the law member of the court who is supposed to be someone versed in military law. There is a court reporter who takes down all questions and answers, and objections of attorneys. A soldier, designated as a Trial Judge Advocate is the Prosecutor. Usually he is skilled as he has performed many previous trials. This was the case in Nelse's trial. It took place in a large room which had probably been the recreation room of a French military barracks. The prisoner, Nelse, was brought in by a Corporal of the Military Police, who, of course, was fully armed. The court swore the Court Reporter to do his

34

duty, swore the witnesses to tell the truth, and the trial commenced with the openings of the Trial Judge Advocate who read the charge against Nelse to the Court. He then made the following opening statement to the Court:

Gentlemen of the Court, this is one of the most important trials that has been held in France. The charge against this defendant is that he and his comrade, Sole, raped this young lady, who is sitting on my right. The lady beside her is her mother, who will also be a witness in this case. Yvette, the prosecuting witness, will testify that Nelse and Sole, on the date of the commission of the offense, forcibly raped her. Her mother will testify concerning her torn undergarments. Yvette, at the time of the commission of the offense, was eighteen years old, and was a virgin.

Gentlemen of the Court, we shall prove each element of the charge and specification in this case, and will demand the death penalty. We are in France, aiding our great ally. We must maintain discipline in our Army, and have the respect of the French people."

In *my* opening statement, I told the Court that my client had pleaded innocent of the offense; that he would testify as a witness in his defense.

The Record of the Courts-Martial

Yvette ———, being questioned by the Trial Judge Advocate, testified as follows:

My name is Yvette ———. I am eighteen years old, and unmarried. On September 14, 1944, I was on my way to my home from the Village of Sur. I saw a colored American soldier standing guard beside a small country road, and stopped to talk to him. He knew very little French, and I didn't know much English, although I had studied it in high school and wanted to try it out. Then two soldiers came along in a Jeep, and stopped and asked me to ride. They looked like nice boys, and I said I would ride as far as my home, which was about a mile up the road, with them. They drove into a side lane, and they both raped me. I fought them, and they tore my clothes. I went home crying, and told my mother."

Yvette was young and pretty. I could tell she had duly impressed the Court. I knew to cross-examine her would be dangerous, but I must try.

35

"Yvette, you have told the Court you fought the soldiers to prevent them from raping you. Did you scream?" "No, I didn't. I didn't think anyone could hear me."

"Were you bruised or injured?" "No, I was not seriously hurt—only my feelings—I cried."

"Yvette, what punishment do you think these soldiers should have?" "Well, I think they should be sent to the front."

"Do you believe that they should be put to death, or given a long prison term?"

"No, I think they should just be sent to the front."

The next witness was Yvette's mother, a large buxom woman, who it was obvious was familiar with worldly affairs.

"I am Cosette, and am the mother of Yvette. My daughter is eighteen years old. She came home on the evening of the 27 of September, 1944. She was crying, and her clothes were torn. She said she had been raped by two American soldiers. I called the police. He took us to the Army place up the road. Yvette pointed out the soldiers—it was him." She pointed to Nelse, and also identified Sole, who was brought into the room.

The Cross-examination.

Q. Mrs. ———, did you take your daughter to a doctor? Answer: No.

Q. Mrs. ———, did you make a claim to the American Claims Office, in Nancy, France, for the sum of ten thousand ($10,000) American dollars as damage for the alleged rape of your daughter?

A. Yes.

And now a loud, "No," from the law member of the Court: "Major Mason, you had no right to ask such a question. Mr. Trial Judge Advocate, you should have objected to that question. Mr. President, you should strike the question and answer from the record of the Court."

Major Mason: No, Your Honor; no. Both the question and answer were proper, Your Honor, for the reason that the same show a motivation for the prosecution of the defendant, and certainly go to the credibility of the testimony of both of the witnesses.

The President of the Court: Upon the advice of the law member, the question and answer are stricken from the record.

The defense counsel: Objection and exception,—the effect of which was to keep the question and answer in the record.

Now Major ———, the law member, was getting angrier by

36

the minute. He stated: "You have no right to bring such testimony into this hearing."

I now excepted in the record to his remarks, which caused him to flush, and say: "Major Mason, you are not aiding in keeping discipline in the U.S. Army."

I replied I was going to do my duty to protect the legal rights of the man I was defending. Again I knew that I was losing to the law member and the Courts-Martial, and must continue to make a good record for the future review, after my client had been convicted.

The Trial Judge Advocate now announced that he had rested his case.

Now came the great struggle. The law presumes a man innocent, until proven guilty beyond all reasonable doubt. That is the English law, and the American law. Yet now we were on foreign soil, in an Army Court. Would the same rules apply? Would the great fear of losing face cause five American officers to again sentence these two soldiers to death?

France, in 1945, was a much different country from what it is today. The great DeGaulle had not then denounced us in public. He had not then ordered NATO from his country. He had not then attended the Quebec Fair. Charles, the Grand, was not yet in control in France. Many American soldiers were yet to die fighting Germans so that France could once again proclaim itself as a world power.

The five American officers sitting as judges of Nelse held the French in awe, respected them; and many soldiers thought their officers tried to court favors from the French. I felt my case was lost before these five members of the Court, but I must make the record. The record must speak the truth for these men. Suppose they had committed the crime for which they were charged, should they be executed, or confined for many long years? These thoughts ran through my mind as I called Chaplain Moran as my first witness.

Q. Chaplain, state your name, age, and occupation?

A. I am a duly ordained Priest in the Paulist Order of the Catholic Church, and am forty-one years old.

Q. How long have you been a Chaplain in the U.S. Army?

A. Since January 2, 1941.

Q. What did you do before that?

A. I became a Priest in 1927. Thereafter I served as a Father Confessor with the Paulists in the University of

37

California, the University of Arizona, and at West Virginia University. I was a missionary to China for nine years, and left there in 1941 and returned to the States and entered the armed forces.

Major Jones, the law member of the Court: "I think we can let the record show that Father Moran is a Chaplain in the U.S. Army."

Defense counsel: "Thank you, Major Jones!"

Q. Father, to what organization are you now assigned or attached?

A. To the 86th Infantry Division.

Q. Are you acquainted with Private Nelse?

A. Yes.

Q. How long have you known him?

A. For more than two years. You see, I first became acquainted with Nelse and Sole during the Louisiana maneuvers. Both these fine men attended mass regularly. They still did, until they were put in jail. It's really a shame these soldiers should be treated the way they have been.

"I move the last remark be stricken from the record," the Trial Judge Advocate shouted. "Strike it," the law member also shouted to the President of the Court. Exception noted by defense counsel.

Q. Father, have you been continuously assigned to the same organization with Nelse and Sole, and served with them since the Louisiana maneuvers in 1942?

A. I have.

Q. What battles and campaigns have you participated in, along with Nelse and Sole?

A. We made the invasion in North Africa; and then we were on the second wave in Anzio. We came into the line in France in December, 1944, and went into the line near the Moselle River during the so-called Battle of the Bulge.

Q. Chaplain, have you been personally acquainted with, and have you personally observed Nelse and Sole during the time you have served as their Chaplain during the past two years?

A. I have.

Q. Chaplain, are you acquainted with the other members of the organization to which Nelse and Sole belong?

A. I am.

Q. Chaplain, will you tell the Court whether or not you are familiar with the reputation of Nelse as to whether or not he has been a law abiding citizen?

38

A. I am.

Q. What is that reputation?

A. It is excellent. To my knowledge, both of these boys have been excellent, brave soldiers. I know one of them—I believe it's you (he looked at Nelse) was awarded the Silver Star at Anzio, where, at night, under heavy fire from German machine guns, he crawled through barbed wire and rescued his wounded Lieutenant. Anzio was terrible. It's a wonder any of us are alive. I buried soldiers there fifteen hours a day. These soldiers regularly attended mass when they could. They were devout. Again I say, I don't believe they would do what this girl says they did!

This time the Trial Judge Advocate didn't have time to object. The law member, Major Jones, yelled: "Chaplain, don't express your opinion."

Major Mason: He has a right and a duty to express his opinion. How else can the record reflect who and what this defendant is?

Law Member: Major Mason, I am warning you! You may be on trial after this case is over for your ungentlemanly conduct.

Major Mason: "No doubt. Let's prefer charges against each other.

Colonel Zinn, the President of the Court: "Now, gentlemen! Let's maintain order."

Major Mason resuming examination:

Q. Chaplain, you have told this Court that in your opinion Nelse has a good reputation among his fellow soldiers and his officers in his Command as a law abiding citizen.

A. Yes.

Q. Now, Chaplain, tell this Court whether or not you are familiar with the general reputation of Nelse among those who know him in his organization for truth and veracity?

A. I am.

Q. What is that reputation, good or bad?

A. In my opinion both Nelse and Sole are truthful men, and again I say I don't believe they are guilty.

Now the Major's face was blue, and he really exploded: "Chaplain," he screamed, "it is for us to decide on the guilt of this soldier!"

Chaplain Moran: "I don't like the way these men have been treated, and I wrote to General Eisenhower and told him so."

Again the law member almost blew his top, and yelled: "Strike that from the record, Colonel."

Again I excepted, and the record contains the statement. Now I had firmly established in the written record that both these soldiers were law abiding, truthful men. This should, under our law, create in the minds of the Court a reasonable doubt as to the guilt of the boy. It would have created such a reasonable doubt before a civil jury, in a civil court. But here I knew the Court had determined what it would do, and had probably been so instructed before the trial commenced. Such was the way of those that administered military justice in 1944, in a theatre of war.

Next I called the defendant, Nelse.

Q. Please state your name, age, and occupation?

A. N———; age, 19; Private Company A, 156 F.A. Bn. U.S.A.

Q. How long have you been in the armed forces?

A. Since June 30, 1942.

Q. Were you drafted, or did you enlist?

A. I enlisted.

Q. Where have you spent your time during your services in the armed forces?

A. Fort Sam Houston, Texas, Louisiana, North Africa, Anzio, Rome, Italy, and now here in France.

Q. Have you been wounded?

A. Yes, I was shot through the shoulder at Anzio, and I received a shrapnel wound in France.

Q. Have you received any decorations or citations from the Army?

A. Yes, sir, I have been awarded two Purple Hearts and the Silver Star.

Q. Where does your family reside?

A. In Boston, Massachusetts.

Q. Who are the members of your family?

A. My mother, who is a widow, one brother, and three sisters.

Q. Do any of them know of this trouble that you are in?

A. I hope not, sir.

Q. Nelse, have you ever been in any trouble with the law in civilian life?

A. No, sir.

Q. Now, Private Nelse, you have heard the charge and specifications read to you, both before and during this hearing, and I believe you have personally pleaded not guilty to the same?

A. Yes, sir. I am not guilty of these crimes.

Q. Now, Nelse, I want you to tell this Court, in your own words, what took place between you, Private Sole, and this young lady?

A. Sole and I had been sent to Bn. Headquarters, and were returning. We saw her (pointing to Yvette) talking to a colored soldier. We slowed down, and I thought she waved. I stopped, and we invited her to go for a ride. She smiled, and got in the Jeep. She spoke some English, which I didn't altogether understand. I didn't speak any French. I drove up into a hedgerow and started to make love. I thought it was all right with her. We got out of the Jeep and had intercourse. Then Sole was with her. Then we drove her up the road, and she got out of the Jeep at her house.

I told her where we stayed at the edge of the little town down the road. That evening she and her mother came, with the Military Police, and we were arrested. That was eight months ago, and I have been in jail ever since.

Q. Did you rape Yvette?

A. No, sir.

Q. Did you abuse her in any other abnormal sexual acts?

A. No, sir.

Q. You are under oath?

A. Yes, sir.

Q. This is your second trial?

A. Yes, sir.

Q. And you were sentenced to death for the alleged offense in the first trial?

A. Yes, sir.

Q. And you were under such sentence for more than eight months?

A. Yes, sir.

Q. And you still say that you are not guilty of the crime?

Major Jones, the law member: "Don't ask the witness the same question over and over again."

Major Mason: "I just wanted to be certain you gentlemen understood the soldier's denial of guilt—just so there wouldn't be any misunderstanding!"

Major Mason: Q. How much education have you had, Nelse?

A. Two years of high school, sir, before I entered the Army.

41

Q. Nelse, is there anything I have omitted to ask you, or that you want to say to the Court?

A. Only, sir, I am not guilty of rape and those other things. She got in our Jeep, went with us, and I thought it was O.K. by her.

Cross-examine.

Now was the Trial Judge Advocate's opportunity, and he questioned Nelse as to every detail of the affair. Didn't he know he was in France? Didn't he know Yvette couldn't speak English? No, Nelse stated, he did not know this, for she willingly got into their Jeep. She smiled at them. She did not seem to be afraid. She was talking freely to a soldier when they picked her up. She looker older than she now says she is. True, she did not demand money, as many other French girls had. She did not seem angry when they let her out of the Jeep near her home.

However, the Trial Judge Advocate shouted and yelled the questions over and over again to Nelse. One could see that the members of the Officers' Court were duly impressed. This same Trial Judge Advocate had tried many cases before this same group of officers, and they thought highly of his skill. Over and over again Nelse stated he was not guilty. Nelse was pale and nervous. It was plain the ordeal of an American boy, having been sentenced to death by one Court, and awaiting execution for eight months, and another trial wherein the death penalty was being sought, was beginning to tell upon his physical wellbeing.

Finally the learned Trial Judge Advocate said, "That's all," and then the law member of the Court, Major Jones, commenced:

Q. Soldier, why did you stop and pick up this girl?

A. I thought she wanted to ride up the road.

Q. Now you know you have not told the truth, don't you?

Before Nelse could answer, I was on my feet, objecting. In a civilian court, I would have demanded a mistrial. But here before this military tribunal, all I could do was protest and object.

Again the Major law member spoke of the undue hardship he was experiencing in maintaining discipline among the soldiers of his division. (I understood why.)

Now came Lieutenant Colonel C. Albright.

Major Mason: Q. Please state your name, age, and occupation?

A. I am Lieutenant Colonel Charles G. Albright, Battalion Commander, 81st Division, U.S. Army. The Army is my career.

42

I was graduated from the United States Military Academy, West Point, Class of 1938. I am thirty-six years old.

Q. Are you acquainted with Nelse and Sole?

A. Yes, sir, they are members of Charley Company, my Battalion. They have been in my organization since the Louisiana maneuvers in 1942.

Q. Tell the Court what type of soldiers Nelse and Sole have been, basing your answer upon your personal knowledge and observation of these men?

A. In my opinion, both of them have been good, brave soldiers. I have regarded them highly. Nelse's Company Commander, whose life he saved when he rescued him from a highly dangerous position at Anzio, recommended him for the Silver Star. This I concurred in, and the award was made. They have both been in battle, both wounded, and both are good men. I've missed them, and needed them badly during the past weeks.

Q. Where is your headquarters now?

A. We are engaging the Germans near ———.

Q. Colonel, tell the Court whether or not you are generally acquainted with the men in your Battalion?

A. I am acquainted with the old timers. I mean by that the men who came with us from the States in 1942. You see, our Division has seen combat action from Africa to Anzio, and now here. Our casualties have been very high. We have had many replacements, and there are many new men whom I am not as personally acquainted with as I am Nelse and Sole. Yes, I would say I am generally acquainted with them.

Q. Are you acquainted with the reputation of Nelse and Sole in your organization for being law abiding, truthful men?

Objection by the Trial Judge Advocate.

The law member would sustain the same, for the reason the question was not properly worded.

Major Mason: Q. Colonel, I want you to tell this Court the reputation this man enjoys among his fellowmen in your organization as to whether or not he has been a law abiding man, and whether or not he is considered to be a truthful man? This will be your opinion, based upon all the facts you have concerning this soldier.

A. In my opinion Nelse is highly regarded by the men in his Company. He is generally pointed out to new men as the one who saved Captain Brown's, his Company Commander's, life. He is highly skilled in map reading. He is an excellent man on

43

night patrols. He was well liked by all—morale has suffered some since he has been in this trouble.

There was no cross-examination of Colonel Albright by the Trial Judge Advocate, or the law member.

The next witness was Captain Charles Brown.

Major Mason: Q. Please state your name, age, and occupation?

A. I am Captain Charles Brown, Company Commander, 81st Infantry Division, the U.S. Army.

Q. How long have you been a member of the organization?

A. Since August 4, 1941.

Q. Are you acquainted with Nelse and Sole?

A. Yes, sir. They are members of my Company. I've known these soldiers personally since the Louisiana maneuvers. Nelse here probably saved my life at Anzio when he rescued me at night, when I had been shot and was unable to even crawl. I recommended him for the Silver Star, which was given to him. He and Sole are among the oldest combat men in my Company, who have been with my company since North Africa. I consider both these men excellent soldiers. They have both been wounded, but to my knowledge they have not shirked or complained. I'm sorry to see them in this trouble. I need them in my Company. We miss them.

Q. Captain, tell the Court whether or not, to your knowledge, Nelse and Sole have ever been in any trouble before the present trouble?

A. None, to my knowledge.

Q. Captain, you, of course, are acquainted generally among the men in your Company, and in your Battalion?

A. Yes. But, of course, we have been having heavy casualties, and are getting replacements from day to day.

Q. Are you acquainted with the general reputation of Nelse among the men in his organization for being a law abiding, truthful man?

A. I am.

Q. What is that reputation, good, or bad?

A. I would say excellent.

"That's all, Captain."

Cross-examination by the Trial Judge Advocate:

Q. Captain Brown, will you name some of the soldiers in your organization who have said Nelse has a good reputation, as you have stated?

44

A. Oh, I just can't say any of them have said the words used here, but after you have lived with men for almost two years in a war, and with men in combat like my men have been, you soon know who is respected and who is not. This I know: both of these soldiers are held in high regard among their fellow soldiers. Many times when I needed men to volunteer to make night patrols, Nelse and Sole stepped forward. I could always depend on them.

It was obvious that Major Jones, the law member, was being disturbed; and the Trial Judge Advocate stated, "no further cross-examination."

The next witness was Sergeant Jones. He stated that he had been in the same squad with Nelse and Sole since the activation of the Company after the Louisiana maneuvers; that his immediate superior, Lieutenant Elliott, had been killed in action last week near St. ———, France.

Q. Sergeant Jones, tell the Court whether or not you are acquainted with the general reputation of Nelse among those who know him in your organization as to whether he is considered a truthful, law abiding man?

A. Yes, sir, I know he is not a liar, and I know he ain't been in no trouble in the Army! I also know the boys who know Nelse and Sole don't believe they went around raping French girls. They didn't have to!

The Trial Judge Advocate almost jumped to the ceiling, and the law member, Major Jones, yelled: "Soldier, only answer the questions asked you."

The usual motion to strike from the record was made by the Trial Judge Advocate, and after much wrangling the trial continued:

The next witness for the defense was Sole.

Major Mason: Q. Private Sole, state your name and rank?

A. Private S——, Company A, 81st Infantry Division.

Q. How old are you?

A. Twenty-one, sir.

Q. How long have you been in the armed service?

A. Three years, sir. On February 1st I volunteered for duty, and was not drafted.

Q. Where have you served in the Army?

A. Fort Sam Houston, Texas; then in the Louisiana maneuvers; shortly thereafter we came to England; from England we invaded North Africa. Then we went to Anzio, in Italy. I was

45

wounded in Anzio, and when I got back to my regiment, they were in France. I've been in France since. I have been in jails for the past eight months, along with Private Nelse.

Q. Now, Private Sole, I want you to look at the Court and tell them just what happened between you and Yvette last year?

A. Yes, sir. Nelse and I were returning from Battalion Headquarters in a Jeep. We saw her (indicating Yvette) talking and laughing with a colored soldier, who was on guard. We stopped and asked her to ride. She smiled, and got in the Jeep. She sort of sat on my lap. Nelse was driving, and he pulled in a lane near some hedges. We both had sexual relations with her. We did not rape her. I thought she was willing, and I still think so. That night she came to Company Headquarters with a woman who I later learned was her mother, and after pointing us out in a lineup, we were arrested and put in jail. We were tried once, if you call it a trial. We didn't have any witnesses, nor did we go on the stand, because the Lieutenant said it would be best that way. Then they said we were guilty of rape and some other terrible offense sexually, and we were ordered hung. During the last six months we were in a French jail under military guard. I expected every day to be taken out and put to death. But I guess General Eisenhower thought we did not have a fair trial, and told them to give us a new one.

Q. Private Sole, tell the Court whether or not you and Nelse raped Yvette?

A. No, sir, we did not. We had sexual intercourse with her, but we did not rape her.

Q. Have you been in any trouble in civilian life, before coming into the Army?

A. No, sir; none.

Q. Have you been in any trouble before this in the Army?

A. No, sir; none.

Q. What rank did you and Nelse have in your Company, before the last trial?

A. We were both Master Sergeants, sir.

Q. What decorations have been awarded you?

A. I was awarded the Bronze Star in Africa, and I have a Purple Heart given me when I was wounded in hand-to-hand combat with a German soldier in Anzio. He stabbed me in my left shoulder with his bayonet.

Q. Did Nelson rape Yvette, the prosecuting witness, at the

time and place set forth in the specification and charge, for which he is now being tried?

A. No, sir, he did not.

Cross-examination by the Trial Judge Advocate:

Q. Private Sole, you are also charged with the same offense Private Nelse is charged with; correct?

A. Yes, sir.

Q. You do admit picking up this young lady, driving her to a lonely place, and having sexual relations with her?

A. Yes, sir; but she seemed willing.

"That's all."

The next witness called was Colonel Pierre Pompando, of the 1st French Army.

Major Mason: Q. Please state your name and age?

A. I am Colonel Pierre Pompando. I am a member of the 1st French Army, and am forty years of age, and at present am on detached duty as a liaison officer to the Staff of the Seventh Army here in Luneville.

Q. Colonel, what was your occupation or profession in civilian life?

A. Before the Huns over-ran my country, I was a lawyer, and had been such for eighteen years in the City of Dijon, France. I was the Prosecuting Attorney there for five years before the war.

Q. Colonel Pompando, are you familiar with the criminal statutes and laws of France? I believe you called it the Code Napoleon until a few years ago?

A. Yes, I am.

Q. Colonel, did I consult you a few days ago, and show you the charge filed by the U.S. Army against Nelse and Sole, being the charge that Nelse is now being tried on?

A. You did, Major.

Q. Did I request you to examine the same, and determine the maximum punishment that could be meted out under the laws of France, if Nelse and Sole were being tried in a French Court for an identical offense?

A. You did.

Q. Tell this Court the maximum sentence these men could receive in a French Criminal Court, if they were to be convicted of this identical crime?

A. A maximum sentence of seven years in prison, and a small fine, Major Mason.

The Trial Judge Advocate moved to strike the testimony of the French Colonel, who was a lawyer in civilian life, from the record; but was overruled by the President of the Court, who made the ruling without consulting with the law member. I've always thought he did so, because he was afraid of offending the French Colonel. To have stricken such testimony would, no doubt, have greatly offended the Frenchman, who was not familiar with our legal procedure.

This was all—not all the case, but all the witnesses.

One of them had remained during the whole trial. Father Moran looked at me and raised his hand with the thumb up. I supposed he had learned that gesture in England from Churchill. I did not feel so jubilant. I knew we would have won our case in a civil court. This was no rape—no screaming woman—no injured female—a smiling young girl who said, I think they ought to be punished by being sent to the front. This was eight months ago. No child was on the way. Mamma had made her claim for ten thousand dollars to our generous Claims Commission. But now I knew the worst was not over. The five officers of the Court had been appointed by the General who had signed one death warrant. They were his officers. He could govern their future careers, promotions, leaves, transfers from staff to combat. They would not disappoint their General if they could help it.

It was late in the day. If I could get the Court adjourned until tomorrow, I would have more time to prepare my argument. I requested the same, but even before the Trial Judge Advocate had an opportunity to make his position known, the President advised me they would conclude the case today, that we could each have one-half hour to make our summation or argument of the case.

In civilian Criminal Courts, the Prosecuting Attorney opens the closing argument or closing summation, then the attorney for the defense makes his argument; and the Prosecuting Attorney closes the case with his argument.

The purpose of a closing argument is to discuss the evidence heard by the Court, and to discuss the law. The prosecutor in civilian courts must not express his opinion upon the guilt of the individual on trial; in fact, appellate courts have reversed many trials because of errors committed by prosecuting attorneys saying, "In my opinion the defendant is guilty." Under our Anglo-Saxon American law, only the jury expresses its opinion when it

48

renders its verdict or findings as to the guilt or innocence of the individual being tried.

Usually in Courts-Martial trials the Trial Judge Advocate outlines his argument briefly to the Court, reserving his "big guns" for the closing.

This was not to be the case here. The Trial Judge Advocate, Captain ———, was a graduate of Harvard Law School, magna cum laude. He had practiced law with a large New York firm for five years before he was called into the U.S. Army, he having been a reserve officer from student army days. He was brilliant, an excellent public speaker, a fine looking young man about thirty-six years old. He had a good knowledge of the law. He was exceptionally proud of his record of more than one hundred trials as a Trial Judge Advocate, without, as he proudly boasted after a drink or two at the Officers' Club, "ever having lost a case before an Army Courts-Martial." He was known by all the members of this Court, and had tried many cases before most of them. You see, the Army in World War II had officers who were carefully selected for Courts-Martial cases, and spent a great deal of their time performing such duties.

Colonel Smith, the President of this Court, had been a classmate of General Patch at West Point in 1919.

Lieutenant Colonel Brown had served in General Patton's Command in the past four years. He frequently returned home to the States as a courier for the General.

Major King, the law member, was the Staff Judge Advocate of the 98th Division, which was attached to General Patton's Army as a Supply Group.

Captain Kuhn had served in the Intelligence section of the General's Army for four years. The General had recommended him for Officers' Candidate School in Louisiana in 1942, and now he held the rank of Captain.

The fifth member of the Court, 1st Lieutenant Duncan, had once been the General's Jeep driver, before he was given a battlefield commission by order of the General shortly after the invasion in 1943.

So you see this Court was not only interested in the guilt or innocence of Nelse, but was also interested in preserving the honor of General Patton.

Those things the Trial Judge Advocate knew, because he was a part of this pseudo legal system.

49

As he arose, smiling, he said, "Gentlemen of the Court, you have a high duty to perform, that of upholding the great tradition of the United States military system, that of maintaining discipline in the great United States Army, and that of showing to the great French people that we honor and respect them. Gentlemen, upon behalf of the United States Government, upon behalf of the American Army, and upon behalf of our great leader, General ———, I apologize to this fine, graceful young lady, Yvette, and to her gracious mother.

"This was a dastardly crime"—he raised his voice and pointed to Nelse—"you savagely committed against this girl, and you should hang for it. You come into France with an Army of Liberation, an army trained to free an enslaved people who had lived under the despotic power of the German beast, and now you have shown yourself to be worse than one of them."

Of course I was on my feet and objected, but I was powerless, for the law member had ruled that the arguments would not be recorded.

Again pointing to Nelse, he screamed: "You are guilty. You lied to this Court. Your fellow soldier Sole lied, because he knows he will eventually hang along beside you. You and he are the despoilers of virtue and womanhood. Don't think for one minute this fine group of officers will be taken in by your lies. You have no testimony corroborating you—only that of a guilty accomplice."

Now he turned to the Court, and said: "Gentlemen, in the name of honor, virtue, womanhood, your daughters and wives at home, convict this man. Convict him, and by doing so, say to the great people of this great nation of France, we respect you."

Perspiration streamed down his face, and he took his seat.

The Court did not smile when I arose and complimented the Captain upon his eloquence and his great speech; in fact, it appeared to me that they were anxious to get on with their business of convicting Nelse.

I knew now I must not pull any stops, but must at least shame the members of this tribunal, in order to save my client's life.

Gentlemen of the Court: "This is no ordinary duty you have been called on to perform. This is a duty that challenges the strength and courage of brave men. Your manner of dealing with this case is a challenge to the American way of life. This is not a case wherein you make a finding and say, 'we leave the

50

results to someone else who may review this case.' This is a case that your conduct in will live long after this war is over and you return to your homes. This case presents not only the issue of innocence or guilt of this soldier, but determines whether men engaged in war, as we are, have the courage to follow the rule of law that has made ours a great nation. Ours is a nation of laws; not a government of men. The rule of law must be followed, if governments survive.

"You gentlemen are the triers of the facts. The issue in this case is whether or not Private Nelse forcibly raped Yvette. She says he did. He says he did not. Private Sole, who was with him, says he did not.

"What supporting testimony does the prosecution have, upon which it attempts to support this conviction?—the testimony of Yvette, who came in crying, and told the story to her mother. Could Yvette have had a motive for this? Had she experimented in the Garden of Eden, and now feared she was pregnant? Were her clothes torn? Did she scream? Did she bite or scratch Nelse or Sole? Gentlemen, were there any marks of battle on them, or on Yvette, a few hours after the affair took place that evening, when they were arrested? Remember, Gentlemen, this charge is forcible rape; not did this man have sexual relations with this girl.

"Mamma was greatly disturbed. She, no doubt, had a right to be; her daughter might be pregnant. She must find the soldiers and see that they were identified and arrested. Then what does she do? The very next day she seeks out the American Claims Officer, and files a ten-thousand-dollar claim for damage to her daughter. Quite thoughtful of Mamma! What a handsome dowry this would make for some young future son-in-law. As the great Tennyson said: 'The jingle of the guinea heals the hurt that honor feels.' No doubt good Mamma of Yvette knew the great French people we had been trying to liberate from the bestial Huns, so ably described by the learned Trial Judge Advocate, had been collecting thousands of good American dollars for every grape vine trampled by an American soldier's heel, as he pursued the Hun through France, every window broken, every roof damaged, and even pay to the French peasants for the rental of the space we buried our dead American soldier boys in."

The law Major was shaking his head. I looked him in the eye, and said: "You know, sir, what I've said is true, and you, sir,

51

and each member of this Court knows that if the lure of that ten thousand dollars influenced the testimony of Yvette, or her mother, you should disregard it entirely.

"Now what does Yvette say to the learned Trial Judge Advocate before he demanded the death penalty of Nelse at your hands? 'How do you think your attackers should be punished?' Her answer: 'I think they should be sent to the front.' Does that sound like the hatred of a girl whose body has been raped and ravished?

"Now what testimony do we have to strengthen the testimony of Nelse? The only testimony lonely men could hope for in a strange land; they seem to have one friend that could aid them. All others, because of war, could not aid them,—Chaplain Moran. Oh, yes, he did write to General Eisenhower, soliciting aid for them. Yes, he went out of channels, and may be Court-Martialed for doing so. But thank God for a man of his courage! Through him we obtained the testimony of the entire group of the commanding officers of the organization to which these men had been attached for the past two years. And what do they all say? Why the best evidence in the world—that Nelse was an excellent soldier, that he had a good reputation as a law abiding man. What better evidence could there be for a soldier, or any man? Under the law, you should give this testimony great weight.

"You should consider how the man has suffered—more than eight months under a death sentence in a jail, in a strange land, away from home; no one to help him but a lone Catholic Father.

"Now the Trial Judge Advocate says: "Put him to death, to preserve discipline in our Army; put him to death to show the great French people that we respect their high standards; put him to death to uphold our great General.'

"Gentlemen, only time will tell what we are accomplishing in this great war. Again I come to the rule of law. This man under our law is presumed innocent, until proven guilty beyond all reasonable doubt. There is a doubt in this case, a reasonable doubt that he committed the crime of forcible rape. If you believe he did, then you may find him guilty. Under the military law, forcible rape is punishable with death, or as a Courts-Martial may determine.

"Surely, gentlemen, if you decide to convict this brave soldier, you should not do more than Yvette asks—'Send him to the front.' Surely, gentlemen, you should consider that he has

52

already spent more than eight months in prison. And gentlemen, will you, as American officers, say to an American soldier, twice wounded and decorated with the nation's third highest honor, we find you guilty and punish you far worse for your conduct than the laws of France would have punished a Frenchman, had he committed the same offense? I call your attention to the testimony of Colonel Pompando, the French lawyer who told you in sworn testimony that under the laws of France this soldier, if convicted, could not be sentenced to more than seven years in prison. "Gentlemen of the Court, in closing let me say no man is above the law, and no man is below the law. This is a great test. Does the American Constitution follow the American Flag, and does it reach out across the Atlantic Ocean and protect this American soldier on the battlefield of Europe?"

The Trial Judge Advocate waived his closing argument.

The Court was closed.

Fifteen minutes later they returned with their verdict.

The President of the Court: "You will arise Private Nelse. It is the judgment of this Court that you are guilty of the charges and specifications, and you are, therefore, sentenced to forfeit all pay allowances, and to be confined for the duration of your natural life in such place as the Commanding Officer may designate."

Thus the trial ended.

Somewhere in France, 1944.

I wondered what we were doing to the youth of America. Were we the great liberators? Were we the freedom-loving Americans? Would we destroy America by trying to show the world what great people we were?

A Trip to Paris

On December 31, 1944, the Battle of the Bulge was raging a few miles north of Dijon, France. The Germans were making an effort to break through our front lines and surround our fighting men.

In the early afternoon of that day I was called to the G1 section and instructed to board the evening train and take a large briefcase which I was told contained highly secret document

53

to Paris. My instructions were to deliver it to a high-ranking General in our headquarters in the Majestic Hotel which had only shortly before been vacated by the hated German Gestapo, a group that had punished and killed many French people in and around Paris.

Ordinarily, the trip from Dijon was only three hours; however, due to the destruction of the railroad tracks by the retreating Germans, it consumed almost eighteen hours. Thus, I didn't arrive in Paris until almost noon, 1 January 1945.

I secured army transportation and was soon at the army headquarters and delivered my briefcase to the proper authorities. Now, I was free for one whole week. You see, I had secured a week's leave before I left Dijon.

I immediately went to the Judge Advocate headquarters and met General Betts, who was Eisenhower's legal advisor, and also several other Judge Advocate officers I had known in the States. They were a very friendly group, and arranged quarters for me at a good hotel.

There was much to do and see in the great city of Paris. Much to my surprise, Red Cross buses were available for sightseeing, and for several days I took advantage of them. I visited the Eifel Tower and toured it; also, the tomb of Napoleon. It was a magnificent place—black marble seeming to be inlaid with gold. There beside it was a black casket supposedly containing the body of Napoleon's brother, Jerome, which Hitler had placed there. It was rumored that when Paris fell to the Germans, Hitler stood at Napoleon's tomb gazing at it for more than an hour.

I visited the railroad car which had been used as a surrender place at the end of World War I. I have a picture of Hitler dancing a jig as he visited the car.

There was plenty of evidence that the Germans did not have an easy retreat from Paris after we occupied it as many buildings were marked with bullet holes, and destroyed tanks were frequently seen.

My visit to Paris was shortly after the fall of that great city. The natives were jubilant, and one was treated like a king. Rides on the famous subway, as everything else, were free to the American soldiers. People were dancing in the street and were very happy that the Germans were gone.

I walked the streets for miles and miles and enjoyed the things I had never even dreamed of seeing. In fact, I had never thought until that time I would see Paris—and probably would not have had I not been in our army.

One day when I stopped in the Judge Advocate head-quarters, General Betts said to me, "I'm going out to Versailles to see General Eisenhower. Do you want to come along?" I certainly did. I enjoyed the ride with the General to Versailles, which was several miles. He told me I could tour the palace while he visited with the General. I enjoyed the tour very much. A much decorated Frenchman, who had lost an arm in the defense of his country, showed me around. He spoke English and told me many things about the great palace, which was built by Louis XII, Louis XIII, and Louis XIV. He took me where the treaty ending World War I was signed.

It was a very cold day, but I toured the palatial grounds and had several hours there. I saw the little bowers where Louis XIV had made love to Marie Antoinette. I recalled that when she was told that the Parisians had no bread and were starving, she said, "Let them eat cake." This cost her her head on the guillotine during the French Revolution.

General Betts returned, and we journeyed back to Paris. He invited me to attend a dinner he was giving for General Montgomery. I spent one of the most enjoyable evenings of my life listening to the great men discuss their war experiences.

Then, on a night when my leave was about up, my friends in General Betts' office took to a famous club in the Montmartre area. An excellent time was had by all.

My leave was up and I returned to Dijon.

A couple years later when I was touring with General Eisenhower in the political campaign, I told him about knowing General Betts, and he said, "You know, he died over there." This made me very sad, for he was a fine gentleman and a great soldier.

At the Front

The weather was very cold and sunless that early February day in 1945 when I journeyed from Luneville, France, to the Seventh Army Headquarters, some forty miles to the town of Morhange. I was assigned as the Assistant Staff Judge Advocate of the Twenty-first Corps that was then directing the fighting for the great German industrial city of Saarbrucken. Our headquarters was in what was left of a French military barracks, called by the French, a military casern. A few days before we arrived, it had been occupied by a fighting outfit of Germans. This was a new assignment for me. For many months I had occupied a desk in a safe rear echelon outfit; now I was with an organization that was to be very close to the fighting and sometimes in it.

One of the first men I was to meet who was a member of this group was a Protestant Chaplain by the name of Elson. He was a young and vigorous Colonel in his early thirties. On the day I met him he had just returned from a mission up front where he had been holding religious services for the soldiers. That day he had a very close call, nearly being killed by some Germans who had shot into his car. He visited front line troops every day and was frequently in danger of being killed or captured. I was to get much better acquainted with him in the next few months as our troops fought their way through Saarbrucken, across the Rhine, and through many German cities to the Austrian border. The records of the War Department will show that our Twenty-first Corps of the U.S. Seventh Army was given credit for advancing through Germany for hundreds of miles, taking many cities and capturing almost one-half million German soldiers.

I spent many long evenings with Colonel Elson, and we frequently discussed what we would do after the war was over. I often told him we should both go to Washington, D.C. I then had hopes of going to Congress, but being a Republican in West Virginia, did not get there. I admired his personality, courage, and ability, and I knew he was a great leader. Colonel Edward Elson did make it to Washington. He became pastor of the old National Presbyterian Church in that city. When

General Eisenhower became President of the United States in 1953, he became a member of that church and regularly attended it. Dr. Edward L. Elson was his close confidant and his spiritual advisor during the eight years of his presidency and until Ike's death. Mamie was also his very close friend and a member of his church. He preached General Eisenhower's funeral sermon before a television audience of millions.

Dr. Elson built one of the most beautiful churches in Washington. I am proud to have attended it, and, upon his invitation, sat in his family pew alongside his beautiful wife and his gracious mother. In addition to his other duties, he was Chaplain of the United States Senate. I have sat in the gallery of that august body and watched him open the Senate proceedings with a prayer that becomes a part of the Congressional record. I have also proudly dined with him, his wife and my lovely daughter, Becky, in the Senate dining room. Reverend Edward L. Elson, a brave soldier, a Christian gentleman, and a great humanitarian, had really arrived in Washington. I'm glad we were, and still remain, close friends.

On to Germany

Some six weeks after our arrival at Morhange, the German city of Saarbrucken fell to our soldiers, and the battle for Germany commenced. Now I really began to see war. Each German town was a fort. Hitler was apparently determined to die rather than surrender. We fought through many German towns—through Mannheim where we crossed the Rhine early in March. Near Heidelberg, which had been declared an open city, I stood on a hill above the city on a Sunday morning. It may have been Easter morning, and I watched our artillery shell the German soldiers retreating from that famed university city. Near there, on that Sunday, I saw unburied German soldiers, dead horses, homes wrecked and burning, and thought, "My God, can this be me in a 'civilized' 1945, or am I dreaming?"

On up the beautiful Rhine with its ancient castles, we moved—into Wurzburg, where our old Forty-second Rainbow Division of World War I fame suffered many casualties and were almost driven to retreat. Each day and night was unreal. The German civilians put out white "flags"—sheets, table-cloths, or whatever they had to show they had surrendered. Their soldiers, the vaunted SS and the Hitler Youth, never gave up. We were sniped at during the day, and our men knifed at night. We drove the German civilians out of their homes ruthlessly as evening came and slept in their beds at night. Each night at nine o'clock the Germans sent over at least one plane to bomb and strafe our headquarters—apparently wanting us to know that they knew where we were. On through the beautiful forests of Germany our division fought. We captured Nuremberg and Augsburg, the home of the great Messer-schmidt factory where they made their fast airplanes.

We spent the night in what was left of the Messerschmidt factory in Augsburg, our Air Force having previously done an excellent job of bombarding it. Early the following morning my Colonel and I were ordered to go to Landsberg nearby to collect evidence for the War Crimes Commission on the Lands-berg Prison Camp. Landsberg was one of the first Nazi prison horror camps liberated. It was located near a pine forest and also close to the railroad. We had no trouble locating it because we could see the smoke from burning buildings as we neared the village. The Germans, learning of the approach of our ar-mies, had apparently set out to destroy the evidence of their work, had deliberately set fire to barrack-like buildings, and had burned many sick and disabled alive.

... Others they had tried to "herd" to the railroad, and many bodies dressed in white and blue convict-like suits were found lying in grotesque shapes toward the railroad in the posi-tions in which they had fallen. Later we were to find thousands of dead, packed like sardines in box cars, on the railroad near Munich, Germany.

We were greeted in the camp by a Polish Jew who said he had been a prisoner there for the past six years. He was a very angry, bitter man, and aided us greatly in finding facts and evi-dence of the brutality of the Germans.

We captured the German Commandant of the prison, a hard-boiled, dyed-in-the-wool Hitler disciple, whom we interrogated to a good effect. We found a few live Jews almost completely starved to death. Emaciated bodies of starved human beings

58

were everywhere—in the partly-burned barracks and on the ground for hundreds of yards leading to the railroad.

The Pole led us a mile away into the pine forest, and there we found countless unmarked graves of thousands of dead Jewish people from all over Europe. Many of those people had been starved to death; others died of exposure and disease. I said to my Polish-Jewish guide: "How is it that so many starved to death, yet you appear to have had enough to eat?" He said, "I'll show you." He reached in his pocket and pulled out a handful of human teeth, some filled with gold. "You see," he said, "for the last five years I have been on the burial detail. The Germans made us pull all the teeth of our dead friends to get the gold. I was able to steal a few of them and to take them to the German farmers nearby, and thus saved my life and the lives of some of my friends from starvation."

The Commanding Officer of the prison camp in Landsburg was a hardened Nazi. He pretended to know but little about the camp, saying he was only a soldier doing a soldier's duty.

I said to him, "You have starved hundreds of people in this camp to death." He said, "They died of typhus." "Why, then," I asked, "did you bury thousands of them in unmarked graves?" He snapped to attention, clicking his heels together, giving a Nazi salute, screaming, "Heil, Hitler," and exclaimed: "No Jew was ever fit to be buried on German soil, and never will be."

We interrogated him for most of two days in an old farm house near the partly-burned and destroyed camp, but were unable to get many facts from him about the prison.

I was at the time assigned to a Staff organization, and among our personnel we had a Jewish dentist. The evening of the second day of the investigation, I was discussing the horror camp to a group of fellow officers, and the dentist took me aside and said, "I have something that will make the Commanding Officer of the horror camp talk." I said, "We cannot resort to Hitler tactics." He said, "This won't hurt him; it is only sodium pentothal, or what you call twilight sleep."

The next day at the farm house where our prisoner was confined, the dentist and I told him we were going to give him an injection in his arm, and that it would be necessary to tie him to the table in the dining room. He evidently believed that we were going to inject him with something that would kill him, for again he snapped to attention, giving the Nazi salute and the Hitler scream, saying he was not afraid to die for the German

59

Reich. Reclining on the table, he bared his arm. My dentist friend injected the sodium pentothal, and in a few minutes our hardened Nazi became very docile. We questioned him for an hour or more and learned many facts, including the hiding place of the prison records, which were later used to good advantage in the trial of many Nazis in high places when hostilities in Germany ceased in May of 1945.

The hard man of Hitler was sleeping peacefully on the dining room table when my Sergeant appeared, saying his patrol had captured two former German prison guards who had been sniping at them in the woods surrounding the horror camp. They had discarded their uniforms and were wearing civilian clothes. This, of course, deprived them of soldier status, if the Sergeant's statement was correct.

I ordered him to being them into the farm house and into the room where the Commanding Officer was peacefully enjoying his sleep upon the dining room table.

One German was very tall, more than six feet; the other one was very small. The tall German became very indignant when I ordered him searched. Throwing his papers on the floor, he screamed, "What is this, a Gestapo?" He was apparently familiar with such tactics as he was later found to be a S. S. Officer. Seeing his Commanding Officer on the table with a mark on his arm where the twilight sleep had been injected, his attitude changed; and as he was being tied up to await transportation, he commenced to scream and pray, apparently thinking we were going to kill him, thus showing, to our disgust, the bravery of the much touted German Storm Troopers Hitler had placed his trust in.

The small guard we tied to a chair in the kitchen of the farm house. His shaking in the chair almost shook the kitchen walls.

These were a few of the men I saw that had been killing thousands of helpless Jewish prisoners.

The Final Weeks

We continued our trek through Germany into the mountains of Bavaria to the Austrian border. There on the Danube River I saw the only bridge that had not been destroyed from North Africa, Italy, France, and through Germany. We had completed our mission, and we knew the Germans could not last much longer. We heard of the death of Hitler, and, in a few days, the war was officially over. I had gone to Munich to see my old friend from home, the City Manager, who was now attempting to manage Munich since he was an officer in Military Government. He told me the war was over—this was May 8, 1945. Many towns in Germany were horribly destroyed. The people were frightened and hungry—yet their greatest fear was of the approaching Russians. They would say—"You are going to fight the Rusky's, aren't you?" Our last assignment was the great city of Leipzig. It had been designated as part of the Russian Zone. We had been sent to administer law and order until the Russian Army could come and relieve us.

An infantry division was attached to our organization. They had not been in the hard fighting through Germany, since they had only shortly arrived from the U.S.A. Our headquarters were in an old office building that had been partially destroyed by our bombers. A bleary-eyed youngster, an American soldier not more than eighteen years of age, was brought into my office by two "spit and polish" M.P. Sergeants acting as his guards. He was unshaven, his uniform was dirty and it appeared as though he had slept in it for several days. I addressed him, saying, "Soldier, why did you kill your Company Captain and your First Lieutenant?" "I don't know." He replied, "I would rather have killed my sergeant than anyone I know." He had a strange, faraway look in his eyes. I ordered him to be sent to Belgium for psychological examination before trial. His outfit had been bivouacked just outside the city of Leipzig. He had disobeyed his Commanding Officer and had gone into a nearby village. The following day he was given what the army terms company punishment, and told to work the streets in the company area for two hours each evening for the duration of one week. The weather there in northern Germany was cold in June. His Captain and Lieutenant had built a fire near their tent and were sitting there enjoying the fact that the war had ended. The young soldier took his carbine and killed them both. War does strange things to young men!

A Visit to Berchtesgaden

World War II ended on May 8, 1945. I was stationed in a little town called Schwäbisch Gmünd. We were about fifty miles from Hitler's famous home in Berchtesgaden that had been built and elaborately furnished for him by his admirers and followers in the Nazi Party when it had complete control of Germany.

On May 11 a Major Farmer and I set out to visit it. The home was in southern Bavaria, and when we arrived there many of the high-ranking officers of our army were also there to see the love nest of the great Führer.

We entered the little town of Berchtesgaden and from there proceeded up a hill about two miles into the German Alps. The scenery was marvelous—high mountain peaks could be seen in the distance. Pines and many other beautiful trees lined the roadway.

The German natives appeared to be looting his home, as we saw several carrying chairs and household furniture of many kinds from the house down the mountain road.

When we arrived at the house, it was almost empty of furniture. It had been bombed by our planes and partly burned. I looked for a souvenir, and all I could find was three hand-made hinges that were easily removed from the partly-burned door that led into a large room which had once contained a very huge window from which a beautiful view could be seen of the high mountains and into the valley below. These hinges were in the form of a Nazi swastika—the Nazi party emblem. I still have two of them in my home.

There was a smaller house high on a peak called the Crow's Nest. This, for some reason, had been closed, and we did not get to visit it.

We drove back into the town where we visited a museum that contained great quantities of glass made into birds and various animals. Our soldiers were guarding it to prevent looting.

Then we toured Hitler's private car that was nearby on a railroad track. It was very elaborate. I thought the great man

62

of Germany would have no more use for it as he was reported to be dead in Berlin.

We looked for a place to eat nearby. I entered an ancient hotel. An elaborate spread of wines and liquors was on a large table and much food was being prepared. I asked the MPM in charge if this was an officer's mess. He said no, that General Taylor of the famous 103rd Division, an airbourne outfit, was escorting General Kesselring, the Commanding Officer of the Italian Campaign who had surrendered to him, and that they should arrive shortly from the Brenner Pass.

Upon leaving the hotel, I heard sirens and thus appeared a large group of cars and many high-ranking officers, including General Taylor and General Kesselring. I was just leaving the hotel as they approached the front entrance. I attempted a salute, but as I had a bottle of cognac under my right arm, covered by my field jacket, I gave the salute with my left hand; and no one seemed to notice or care. Proceeding to our base, we saw thousands of soldiers—Germans who had surrendered to our troops.

This was the area called the National Redoubt where Hitler was supposed to make his last stand. Our outfit was credited with taking 350,000 prisoners on our march through.

Back Home at Last

Early in June I was ordered home since I had accumulated the highest number of so-called points of any officer in my organization. The U.S.A. never looked so good as it did when I arrived there in the latter part of July 1945. My Bronze Star, my three Battle Stars, and the handmade hinges in the form of a Nazi swastika which I had taken from Hitler's home in Berchtesgaden are in the den of my home now high on a hill in West Virginia, reminding me of the horrors of war. Since coming home, believing we had ended wars, my oldest son, Tom, has gone through the terrible fighting in Korea, son George has spent a large part of his young life in the U.S. Navy, and now, as I write this some twenty-five years after my return, my tall red-haired grandson, Lou, is wondering when he will have to fight in Vietnam.

I wonder what we have accomplished in my lifetime of wars! World War I—the "war to end all wars"—I remember it. World War II. Korea. Vietnam. What next?

Let's hope the eighteen-year-old voters will send to Washington men to govern us who will have sense enough to keep our great nation out of wars!

A Tribute to G.I. Joe

I've seen Africa's Sunny Clime, Oran, Bizerte, the Arabs and
    the girl called Girty;
I've been to Italy, seen Salerno, Anzio, and Rome.
There was Fieuta Pass—the hills south of Po—
G.I. Joe, they called the soldier man—why?
I do not know.

There's a name for high estate—Presidents, Kings, Senators
    and Governors of State;
To such, men bow! Take off your hats and courtly favors give.

I've seen G.I. Joe, mid shot and shell—that would make the
    very name of Hell sound like a paradise;
I've seen him on the ocean when submarines were round,
Bombers in the sky, strafed and bombed!
But not afraid to die.

I've seen him on strange beaches!
Thru pill boxes, forging a way;
I've seen him upon river banks;
I've watched him cross and die;
I've seen him carrying old glory ere the morning sun was high.

I've seen him free four lands or more,
Restoring nations to a way—called Liberty!
I've seen his graves in many lands,
Crosses marked with numbered bands.
I've seen the palaces of Kings,
Looked upon a crown or two, and Ambassadors I've known—
Presidents, Senators, and Governors, a few.

To me there is a name that will ever, with eternal flame, glow
Above them all. I'm glad I knew you, G.I. Joe.

BOOK TWO

The Law Years

My First Case

About the only law practice a very young-looking attorney, fresh from law school, could get in 1927 was that of representing poor people arrested for possessing that alcoholic beverage called moonshine liquor.

I had opened an office in the Scotts Run section at a place called Osage, West Virginia, and began to practice my profession representing mostly coal miners and the very poor in that depressed year.

Squire Columbus was the Justice of Peace in the village of Osage. He was the law, and he administered it not according to the book, but as he felt it should be.

I had one of my first trials scheduled for 7:30 p.m. before Squire Columbus, whom I had not yet become acquainted with, and proceeded there, very nervous as all young attorneys are with their first case. My client had been arrested by a local constable and charged with the possession of a small quantity of moonshine—less than a pint.

I arrived at the Squire's office about 7:00 p.m. where I had told my client to meet me. I walked into the office and found the Squire alone. He was sitting behind his desk with his feet propped on top and was sound asleep, snoring very loudly. I moved a chair, and the noise I made awakened the Justice. As he awoke he jerked suddenly, and the chair he was sitting in upset, causing him to fall backwards to the floor. He arose as suddenly as he fell and, being slightly intoxicated, yelled at me, "God damn you! You did that! I'm going to put you in jail for contempt of court!"

I was almost frightened to death. "Oh, no, Judge," I stammered, "I just came in to try a liquor case that you have set for 7:30." I introduced myself as Attorney Mason, and he became more calm. I told him the name of my client.

He went into an anteroom and returned with a bottle containing a very small quantity of liquor. The bottle had the name of my client on it. He smelled the contents of the bottle, tasted it, and then drank it all. He then went to a water tap and placed a small quantity of water in the bottle.

"Mason, I hope you win your case," he stated, "you're sort of a nice young feller." I DID!

Coal Mining in Scotts Run During the Early Years

It was a long winding valley between two high hills—the road was hard and narrow. It wound its way along a stream called Scotts Run for some ten miles or more, in Monongalia County, West Virginia.

The year was 1927. Literally hundreds of houses containing from two to four rooms dotted the hills on each side of the road and creek. The only plumbing they contained was a water tap in the kitchen. Toilets called water closets or privies were to the rear of the house and close to the stream in order that the human waste would sometimes be carried down the creek when it was in flood stage.

Rusty yellow sulphur water ran into the creek, coloring the rocks a dull yellow. The sulphur came from mines that dotted the hills on each side of the stream. The stream also contained garbage, old cans, old tires, and empty white whiskey bottles—the product of the Prohibition years. A railroad used exclusively for the purpose of hauling the coal ran along the side of the road through the entire length of the coal mining area. This was the famous Scotts Run Coal Mining Region in 1927.

The Scotts Run section was once beautiful farming country. Cattle grazed in its valleys and hills; corn, wheat, oats and barley were grown. It was considered one of the real beauty spots in West Virginia. Then came World War I and with it the great demand for coal to make steel for war purposes. The coal underlying this region was known to geologists as the Pittsburgh Vein. It was six feet thick, and being low in sulphur content, was superb for making coke, which in turn was necessary for the making of steel.

At the start of 1914, hundreds of people of all nationalities moved into this coalfield. There were Russians, Poles, Italians, miners from Wales as well as England, Lithuanians and Negroes from southern United States. Later, in 1930, several

70

hundred Negroes were imported from Alabama and moved into shanties in a place called the "Patch" to be used as strike-breakers. From 1914 to 1925 there was a great demand for coal.

It has been said that at one time in this Scotts Run coalfield, 147 separate companies were mining in the ten-mile area. In 1918, coal brought a very high price—eighteen dollars per ton. In 1970 it had dropped to six or seven dollars per ton.

The mining methods then were by hand, and a good miner could mine eight to ten tons of coal each day, for which he received a very high wage. The mining methods of that period were very hazardous, and many men were killed and injured in the mines.

Some 2,500 coal miners were employed in the Scotts Run field in 1925. Then the Great Depression commenced in the coal industry. The demand for coal decreased. The companies began to lower the price of coal, and as they lowered the price they of course lowered the wages. Many of the companies closed, others failed and were closed by court proceedings or bankruptcies. Few miners were employed at fixed wages, and if so, they were very small. The companies that continued to operate paid the miners a fixed amount for each ton of coal produced. The amount was so small that a miner who worked in the mine each day from daylight until darkness could not earn enough to feed himself and his family, no matter how small. The coal he loaded was placed in a mine car that was supposed to hold a designated tonnage. This was weighed at the mine portal by an employee of the company called a check weighman. Often, in order to hold his job, the check weighman cheated the miners, thus in effect, robbing him of his wages. Since the coal car was supposed to contain a fixed tonnage, the miner was required to load it almost beyond its limit of containing coal.

As times became harder in the depression, the so-called "Clean-Up System" developed, wherein the miners were required to do extra work, such as setting posts and clearing up rock and mine falls. For this work they received no pay. Work gradually decreased from six days per week to three, and then one and two, and many of the miners became unemployed. Those who worked were forced to deal at the stores owned by

71

the coal companies, and they were charged much higher prices for the commodities they purchased.

The small houses occupied by the miners rented for only a few dollars a month, but soon the unemployed miners could not pay the normal rent and were evicted by the local justice of the peace who, of course, favored the coal operators. It must be remembered that this was all taking place in America before 1932 and, at that time, federal relief and Social Security were unheard of. There were of course some county poor houses, but such places were filled with old people who did not receive monthly Social Security checks. Many of the miners became destitute—hungry and without shelter. Local citizens from the prosperous university city of Morgantown collected stale bread from bakeries and took it to Scotts Run, where often hungry children fought over it. In 1930 some two thousand men, women, and children marched through Granville and Westover toward Morgantown in order to show their plight. Whether or not the rumor was correct that there would be an attempt to raid stores and warehouses for food, I do not know. They were met at the Pleasant Street Bridge, then the only one crossing the Monongahela River, by County Judge Charles G. Baker, reinforced by State Police armed with machine guns. He succeeded in convincing them to turn back with assurance that some relief would be provided for them. They returned to their shacks and hunger. This was our great America in 1930. Coal was still being used by all railroads and by many electric utility companies, but the price was so small that even the large companies were not paying a living wage to their miners who dug the coal.

In early 1925, a young man who had worked in the mines in his native state of Illinois appeared in the Scotts Run Coal Mining area, in Monongalia County, West Virginia, and commenced to organize a union of miners called the United Mine Workers of America. He was the great John L. Lewis.

Meetings were called—first quietly in the homes of miners, and then in private halls and then, later, in public gatherings at public places. The coal operators seemed to control the local papers because a great amount of negative comment began to appear in the press. Lewis and his organizers were referred to

72

as the Industrial Workers of the World, Communists, Socialists, and many other unflattering terms.

The men organized into a union. Most of the success of Mr. Lewis was made possible by the miners' wives, who were bearing the great burden of poverty due to the low wages and unemployment of their husbands. Men who joined the union were refused employment and were blacklisted by the coal companies (placed on a list of undesirables by the companies as not fit for employment). Those who joined the union were also evicted from their homes. Having no place to live, old buildings were rented and then temporary cheap wooden barracks were constructed—all without the facilities we know today. In these temporary shelters, constructed by the union, hundreds of men, women, and children lived through the cold winter and into the hot summer months—with little to eat and no heating or cooking facilities. Many people literally starved. Many died of disease. Violence flared. Properties were dynamited, burned, and destroyed. The coal companies hired men as guards for their properties. These guards were licensed to carry concealed weapons by the local courts.

The miners secured arms, and virtually civil war commenced. Fires burned at night on mine property and mine guards fired guns into homes, in some cases killing children. Local courts issued injunctions against the miners picketing and against John L. Lewis. He was jailed in Monongalia County and released only through the Supreme Court of Appeals.

These conditions continued for a period of almost five years—until 1932, after which time people and the government began to believe labor had a right to combine in organizations called unions for their common welfare.

This was during the period that thousands of miners, attempting to organize their union, armed themselves with guns, knives, and clubs and marched on Cabin Creek in Kanawha County, West Virginia. They seized a passenger train of the C&O Railroad Company, operated it up and down the tracks and fought the West Virginia National Guard, which had been called out to protect the property of the coal operators. Later, many of them were to be tried for treason against the United States. However, thanks to that great union attorney, Tom

Townsend, hired by John L. Lewis to defend them, none were convicted. John L. Lewis was an honest, fearless man. He had labored in the mines as a coal digger. He knew the danger of gaseous mines, falling mine roofs, explosions; and he also knew of the greed of the great coal operators, many of whom lived in luxury on Park Avenue in New York, in Philadelphia and Cleveland, or other cities far removed from their mines. He was determined to improve the living conditions of his union members. He did. He established the right to bargain by the use of strikes. He bargained for, and got, an eight-hour day. No longer would men labor in the mines from daylight to darkness and starve along with their families. No longer would they have only potato peelings and water for their noon lunch while at work. He bargained for and got forty cents for a welfare fund for each ton of coal produced by the operators. This money was to eventually amount to millions of dollars and is being used as pensions for older miners and for medical attention for them and their families.

Union coal miners now average somewhat over one hundred dollars for eight hours' work. Most of them own fine homes, good automobiles, and send their sons and daughters to college. They occupy a high, respected place in their communities, constitute a power in politics, and command the respect that brave working men should have. They stand high in the saddle.

From all this, another group also has prospered—the mine owners. Now great companies own most of the mines. They earn very handsome profits for their stockholders and the coal mines of West Virginia are valued at millions of dollars.

Blasphemy in Monongalia County

Two large families, the Moores and the Tennants, had settled in the early days in what was to become Clay and Battelle districts, Monongalia County, West Virginia. They intermarried, but soon feuds developed between them. They established separate churches and tried to do the same in their schools.

Josiah Tennant was what was then known as a "cattleman." He made his living through buying and selling cattle. He was a very tall man about fifty years of age. He cultivated a very long beard and wore a long, cowskin coat and a coonskin cap. He drank much whiskey, which, it was reputed, was made in a mountain still. He was not a religious man.

The Moores were very devout people and held many church meetings. The churches in those days were lighted by oil lamps and the light was never very bright. Josiah Tennant, on a certain Wednesday, had been to Morgantown and was on his way home by horseback. He had imbibed in alcoholic beverages very heavily. As he was passing the church of his enemies, the Moores, he noticed a light. He got off his horse and looked in the window. He saw many Moores in the dimly-lighted church on their knees praying.

He opened the church door and jumped into the aisle, wearing his coonskin cap, his long coat and his very long beard, and yelled at the top of his lungs, "Arise you sons of bitches, I am the angel Gabriel and this is the Judgement Day!"

He was indicted by the Circuit Grand Jury for blasphemy, but at his trial the humor was so great that the Judge only fined and reprimanded him. Thus, the only trial for blasphemy in Monongalia County was ended.

The Case of Loran Jones

"Prisons do not seem to reform the criminal nor deter the commission of crime." In the year 1935 when I was a young lawyer, along with two other young lawyers I was appointed to defend a young man who had been arrested for murdering a young woman in the mountains of West Virginia. The following is his exact statement freely given by him and is true in all respects, though his name has been changed.

STATEMENT OF LORAN JONES

I am thirty years of age, and was born in Deer Park, Maryland. My mother is living and is sixty-seven years of age. My father died in 1925. In 1924, I was convicted in Marion County, West Virginia, of murder in the second degree, and was sent to the State Penitentiary for the term of eighteen years. After serving six and one-half years, I was paroled. My education was

75

the completion of the third grade in school at Everson, West Virginia. While in the penitentiary, I worked hard every day, even while I was sick and my hands were sore and my record there is clean. The prison life is very hard, and when I left there, I told them I would never be back. I came directly from the prison to Maidsville, West Virginia, where I went to work in the coal mines, and I lived with my mother. There I met Nell Lawton whom I lived with about a year. She pretended to be in love with me. However, we had some trouble and separated; I gave her the furniture that we had. This was in 1930. During the next three years she compelled me to pay her money constantly, threatening to tell the officers that I had violated my parole by crossing the state lines and going into Pennsylvania and Maryland, out of West Virginia. During this time I was constantly in fear of being arrested and suffered a great deal. In fact, I had more peace of mine while in the penitentiary than I have had since I have been out. Yet the prison broke my nerves by working me like they did, and I dreaded to go back.

Nellie informed me that she was in love with another man, and that she was going away with him. She demanded $100.00 from me to go away on. I told her that I didn't have the money, and she stated to me that I would have to suffer the consequences, indicating that she would see the officers and turn me in. I pleaded with her and told her not to do that, stating that I would try to get the money. I went to Mrs. Mascioli and tried to borrow the money, but she would only let me have $40.00 on my watch. I got the $40.00, and met Nellie on the bridge the day of the killing. I told her that I only had $40.00. She said that would be no good, that I would have to get the $100.00, and started to walk away, saying that she would see the authorities. I told her that I had some other friends whom I would try to get the money from, and asked her to get back into the car, which she did.

Driving out through the Cheat Mountains the road was very muddy and my car started to over heat. I started to stop, stating that to continue would only burn up the engine. She said that she would walk. I said, go ahead and walk. She got out of the car and started away; I got out and shot her once. She fell, and I shot her five more times. I then dragged her off the road to a little hollow and threw stones on the lower side of her and covered her up with dirt and leaves. Afterward, I went back to Morgantown, turned my car over to Hardesty, and slept that night at my mother's home. After working the next day at the

76

mines, I drew my money out of the bank and left the following Thursday. I went to Denver, Colorado. I couldn't get any work there, and bummed my way back to Wheeling where I was arrested by the local officers. I was arrested about 2:00 A.M. and was brought back to Morgantown, where I was put in jail. After I had breakfast I was immediately taken to Fairmont to the State Police Headquarters. There I was questioned by the officers, Officer McClung hitting me in the stomach and knocking me out for five minutes. Then some other officer beat me with a hose, showing me a statement made by a brother of one Bill Hardesty. It stated that Bill Hardesty had told his brother that he had helped get the woman and bring her to the hill while I was digging the grave. This was not true, as Bill Hardesty had nothing to do with this.

On January 14, 1935, my attorneys, Kermit R. Mason, William T. Hughes and Charles H. Haden, who were appointed by the court to defend me, came to the jail, where I gave them this statement. Thereupon they advised me that if I plead guilty to first-degree murder, in all probability, the Judge would sentence me to life imprisonment. They further advised me that if I stood trial, I had a bad chance. They felt the jury might find me guilty of first-degree murder, giving me no chance for a recommendation of mercy. Consequently, the Judge would have to sentence me to death. I informed them that the only thing I would plead guilty to would be second-degree murder, agreeing to serve out the balance of my former sentence, approximately twenty-five years. "I would rather be hanged than spend the remainder of my life in the penitentiary, and my attorneys above named are hereby instructed to defend me in every possible legal manner, and I am assuming full responsibility, and will not enter any plea other than a plea of second-degree murder or a plea of not guilty to first-degree murder."

Loran Jones was tried by a jury. He was found guilty and sentenced to life imprisonment. About six years later while serving his sentence in the state prison, he was killed by a fellow prisoner. I have often thought that if he had been sensibly treated in prison, both he and the young woman would still be alive.

77

Some Judges I Have Known:
An Arizona Judge

He came to a little Arizona village in 1919. He was then about forty-five years of age. He was very quiet but friendly, and made a rather good appearance. His wife, somewhat younger, was a beautiful woman, and, in addition, possessed a vibrant, pleasant personality. Soon she was acquainted with most of the people in the village and was actively engaged in most of the social and civic functions. She made many friends and aided her husband in getting established in his law business.

A vacancy occurred in the office of Circuit Judge, and due to his wife's friendly associates, he was elected Judge of the Circuit Court of that county. Soon a change in his previously friendly manner came about. He became very arrogant and domineering with those having business with his court. He quarreled with the Prosecuting Attorney, the Court Reporter, and even with the Sheriff. On one occasion when he was trying a murder case, he suddenly stopped the trial and the following statements were made by him to a crowded courtroom:

"Do you know who I am? Why, I am the Judge of the Superior Court of Pinal County, Arizona. I have the power of life or death over you. I have the power to close all the banks and take over all the business in this county. Sheriff, shoot anyone who creates a disturbance. I carry a pistol, and I know how to use it too!"

He shocked the audience with this conduct. The news soon spread throughout the county. His next move was to employ a character known as an outlaw gunman for his protection. Thereafter, he was seldom seen on the village streets without his bodyguard.

He had a physical encounter with his Court Clerk and arrested him, sentencing him to jail. He also sent his clerk's friends to jail, though their only offense was that of friendship with the Clerk of the Court. He had previously meted out long prison sentences to young men for minor sentences, sending them to the state prison.

The people of the county instituted a recall proceedings and he was removed from the Judgeship. An investigation of his past revealed that for a number of years before coming to Arizona, he had been confined to a mental institution in New York state, and after his release came to Arizona. There he was elected Judge of one of its highest courts. Some years later he was arrested for walking the streets of Chicago almost naked, and after being hospitalized, died.

The following entries are taken from Arizona newspaper accounts of legal proceedings involving the Judge.

May 19, 1924—Judge of Pinal County Superior Court is arrested on charges of carrying a concealed gun.

May 21, 1924—Superior Court of Phoenix holds that Judges are peace officers and therefore can carry concealed weapons.

May 24, 1924—Nine hundred Pinal County citizens sign petitions seeking recall of Superior Court Judge who presides with "pistol in hip pocket, and has a bad temper, suffering from hallucinations."

April 18, 1925—Right of the voters to recall Superior Court Judges for misconduct in office is upheld by State Supreme Court.

June 20, 1925—Arizona Supreme Court reverses ruling that Superior Court Judges are peace officers and therefore are free to carry weapons.

All these are listed in *An Arizona Chronology* published by Douglas D. Martin from "News Happenings in Arizona."

A West Virginia Judge

"I don't give a good hoot about attending any of the meetings, Mason, to hell with them, I just came along for the ride."

Thus spoke Judge Kite, newly elected to the exalted position of Judge of the Circuit Court of a West Virginia County, when we were attending the American Bar meeting in Dallas, Texas.

The Judge of this court was possessed of great power. Among his many duties was the administration of judicial justice in all civil, criminal, domestic, and juvenile cases. His judgment was subject to review only by the Supreme Court of Appeals of the State, and in exceptional cases, by the Federal courts.

In order to have his judgment reviewed by the Supreme Court, one must, at great expense, have the record of his cases prepared by the Court Reporter and the Circuit Clerk, and then journey to the State Capitol to petition the Appellate Court to consider the matter. The Supreme Court in our state consisted of five judges who were elected and being overworked; it was always difficult to get them to consider many cases on appeal. Thus, it can be readily seen that the judgment of Judge Kite was rarely questioned.

Judge Kite was sixty-one years old when elected. His experience as a lawyer prior to his election was very limited. He served as county prosecutor during World War II, and it was said that he tried few cases and lost them all.

He was elected not because of his popularity or ability, but because his predecessor in the Judgeship for the sixteen previous years had become so unpopular due to misconduct in office that he couldn't even carry his own home precinct in the election in which Judge Kite defeated him.

In his campaign for election, he promised to study the law and to diligently follow the rules laid down by the legislature and the courts. Before his election as judge he always abstained from discussing legal propositions, as is the custom among friendly lawyers, by waving his arm and saying, "Why you know more about that than I do," or "You've had more experience than I've had, and you know more about that than I do." This custom he still continued on the bench and usually said to opposing attorneys, "Why, both you fellows know more about this than I do—you've had more practice with the matter."

When he ran for Judge he was totally devoid of clients. He confidentially told me that he only had one large estate to manage and that he was living off of it.

He possessed very few law books—none of them current. He had been unable to rent an office because he did not pay his rent. His office at the time of his election was one dark room which was a common walkway to his landlord's office. It didn't make much difference to him because it was only a place for him to loaf and maybe hope.

Some six years before he ran for Judge he was defeated in an election for Circuit Clerk of the Court, of which he was now the Judge—having been elected for an eight-year term.

The county furnished him with a modern library—and it was hoped that he would use it. He visited neighboring judges—borrowed their grand jury charges and instructions to juries, which he read to each of his juries—verbatim.

He did not study the law. He was too busy. He depended mainly upon the legal knowledge of his court reporter who, though a licensed attorney possessing considerable knowledge of court procedure, had not practiced the profession. The Judge committed many errors and many of his decisions were reversed by the State Supreme Court. Consequently, there was a great drive to clean up the county through the next election.

In the political race, his opponent stated that the Judge was so dumb that it would be necessary to point him towards the Court House in order that he could find his way there. Now, many of us believe that this was true.

He delegated all his appointments by saying, "See my secretary, she will give you an appointment; she will fix the time." This was quite a powerful position for his secretary, able to see the Judge who, when not holding court, was in the next office with the door closed.

Upon one occasion I questioned her power in open court by saying, "Your Honor, you agreed to hear this case involving a suit by a widow against an insurance company on November the 25th, and regardless of the fact that your secretary fixes your docket, you should hear it as scheduled." The Judge confined me to jail for contempt of court. I demanded a hearing—Judge Kite gave me none. However, Kite entered an order signed by himself and placed it in the court records, indicating that I had been tried and convicted.

We have no recall for Judges. They can only be removed by impeachment by the legislature of the state, which is almost impossible. Judge Kite was not re-elected, but our methods of selecting our high Judges must be changed.

The Fox Case

In 1951 Ralph Fox was operating a small coal mine in northern West Virginia. He employed eighteen men, who, by the aid of machinery, daily produced about three hundred tons of

81

bituminous coal. This was considered a very small, insignificant operation in Monongalia County, West Virginia, where it was common for hundreds of men to be employed in the one mine and producing in some cases as much as ten thousand tons of coal each day.

Fox was a long, tall, lanky mountaineer, about forty-five years of age. He possessed the independent pioneer spirit common to mountaineers of West Virginia. In fact, in at least one instance he had been imprisoned by a Federal United States Judge for selling whiskey during Prohibition. Thus he joined that great fraternity of thousands of Americans who were for repeal of the Eighteenth Amendment and ignored the law.

I refer to this, as it is a part of the story of the Fox Case. Ralph, after his time at Lewisburg Federal Prison, where he became acquainted with such notables as Circuit Judge Manton, of New York, who was doing time for accepting hundreds of thousands of dollars of bribes, returned to his home near Morgantown, West Virginia, and became a hard-working, honest citizen. He did not drink intoxicants. He was a shrewd, hard-working business man, very intelligent, and possessed a limited education. He often claimed to be part Cherokee Indian, and he may well have been, as his features suggested the same.

The coal business was very good. Ralph's operation was making money. His men were steadily employed and seemed content. However, a day came, when, because of some small grievance, the men went on strike and refused to work. Ralph hired other men and kept on mining coal.

Then the long arm of the Federal Government stepped in. Fox was notified of a hearing by the National Labor Relations Board, and after the hearing was ordered to reinstate the eighteen men who had quit, and in addition, to hire only Union miners. This Ralph refused to do.

Next he received a very formal notice from the United States Government, informing him that unless he reinstated the eighteen men and hired only Union miners, that his mine would be seized and operated by the United States Government, under the War Powers Act. That was when Ralph consulted me.

I heard his story, read the letters from the government officials, and advised him not to worry, that this was 1950, that

82

we were not at war; that if the government seized his mine which he owned, that they would have to bring a Court proceeding. I read to him the Fifth Amendment to the Constitution of the United States, which provided that property could not be taken or seized, except by due process of law. I further advised him that this meant that the U.S. Federal Government, if they tried to take his property, would be forced to institute a suit in a Federal Court; that if such a suit was brought, we would then appear in the Court and protect his rights. I thought I knew the law, and that I was advising him properly. I little dreamed of what was going to happen.

A few days thereafter, a young man appeared in my office and advised me that he was an attorney in the United States Department of Interior, in Washington, D.C., and that he desired to advise me that unless Ralph Fox obeyed the order of the N.L.R.B. and rehired the eighteen men, and recognized the Union, that his coal mine would be seized by the United States Government and operated by the United States Department of the Interior. I inquired of him as to how the property would be taken. He was vague as to details. He refused to state what Court the proceedings of seizure would be brought in. He volunteered the information that for a number of years after graduating from a Kentucky law school that he had served as an elected Justice of the Peace in Kentucky, and that he was familiar with Court proceedings. I told him to institute his suit, and that we would see him in Court.

The following Monday morning Ralph called me. He was very excited. He said West Virginia State Police with machine guns, a U.S. Navy officer, and others, had physically taken possession of his property, that he had been ordered off the premises, that he had been advised by a man dressed in a Navy uniform, who informed him that he was a Lieutenant Commander in the Navy, that he was taking the property under the authority of the War Powers Act of the United States Government, and that thereafter he would operate it in the name of the U.S. Government, under the branch of the Department of Interior. This I could hardly believe. However, I advised Fox to refrain from violence, and that I would investigate that matter later that day. This I did, and to my dismay found three

Navy officers and several State Policemen in charge of and guarding this small coal mine.

The Lieutenant Commander informed me that his orders were to fire the men Fox had hired, to reinstate the eighteen who had gone on strike, and to operate the mine to produce coal, which was needed in the national economy.

I inquired how Fox was to be compensated for his property, and he informed me that Fox could file his claim with the United States Government, and it would be considered in due time.

Within a few days many men had been employed in and about the mine; in fact, from the large number of employees, Navy personnel, and guards, one would have thought it was a large coal operation. However, instead of the 300 tons of coal Fox had been producing with his eighteen employees, the production dropped to as low as 50 tons per day.

I instituted a suit, with Ralph Fox the plaintiff and The United States of America and the then Secretary of Interior, Mr. Krug, as the defendant.

The suit was brought in the Federal Court of the United States for the Northern District of West Virginia. The bill of complaint which was filed in the Clerk's office in Elkins, West Virginia, alleged that Fox owned a fully equipped coal mine consisting of valuable machinery, supplies and equipment; that parties claiming to be officers and agents of the Federal Government had, by force, and with the use of guns and arms, unlawfully seized Fox's property without due process of law; that he had been deprived of the use and ownership of the same, in violation of his rights under the United States Constitution, particularly the Fifth and Sixth Amendments thereto, and also in violation of the Constitution of the State of West Virginia.

The United States District Judge at that time sitting on the bench of this Court, was an elderly man by the name of The Honorable William E. Baker. He was a fearless Judge. He had been appointed by President Harding. He did not approve of many of the policies of the New Deal commenced by the late President Roosevelt and now being pursued by President Truman. He was the same United States Federal Judge who had sent Fox to Lewisburg for violating the Prohibition Law.

84

The United States Attorney of the Court was the late Joe V. Gibson, a tall, large man, resembling in appearance Abe Lincoln. He was honest. He believed in the rule of law that has made this country a great nation.

Ordinarily such a suit as this could only have been brought in the District of Columbia, where Mr. Krug, the Secretary of Interior, presided. However, we believed the suit could be maintained in our home Court where the property was located, and where the agents of the Government had charge of the mine, basing our rights under a prior decision in a like suit in a Kentucky Federal Court. This we believed was especially true if we could prove waste, destruction and irreparable damages to our property which we were certain we could do.

In our complaint filed with the Court, we asked for a mandatory injunction against the Secretary of Interior and his agents, the Navy Commander, and others, requiring the coal mine and property thereon to be returned to Fox.

The day of the trial arrived. Also arrived from the City of Washington, a battery of United States Special Attorneys, several Navy Officers and others. We were now in Court, in the forum where we expected to be protected by that great document, the United States Constitution.

Mr. Gibson arose and addressed the Court. "Your Honor, I now desire to present for admission to this Honorable Court Mr. Hayden, who is a Special Assistant to the Attorney General of the United States. Mr. Hayden is especially skilled in matters of this sort, and I am not, and he will represent the Government in this case.

Judge Baker: "So you say, Mr. Gibson, that he is skilled in matters of this sort, and you are not. Very well, let the young man come forward. The Clerk will administer the oath, and he may be admitted to practice in this Court."

Mr. Hayden, having been sworn to support the United States Constitution, etc., the trial commenced. Or did it? Thereupon the Assistant to the Attorney General filed many pleas and legal motions to delay the trial. He took the position, and argued ably, that the District Court did not have jurisdiction to hear the case, that the suit could only be brought in the District of Columbia. He maintained further that under the

War Powers Act the Government had the legal right to seize Mr. Fox's coal mine, and that Mr. Fox's only right was to file a claim for the use and damage to his property in the United States Court of Claims in the District of Columbia.

I argued that our property had been seized within the jurisdiction of this Court; that the same was being irreparably damaged; that Fox's constitutional rights were being violated. I showed the Court the precedents, those being like cases in Federal Courts, particularly the Federal Court cases in the same type of case where the United States Government had also seized coal mines in Kentucky.

Judge Baker decided he had jurisdiction, and that he would hear the case, but would hear it in the City of Wheeling, West Virginia, where he also sat as a Federal Judge.

The trial finally got under way. Many days were filled with the taking of testimony. Ralph Fox was the first witness. He testified as follows:

> I am Ralph Fox. I am forty-one years old, and live in Morgantown, West Virginia. I own a small coal mine, where I formerly employed eighteen men. These men quit last July over some grievance which I really never knew the real reason for. I had orders for my coal and had bills to pay, so I hired other men who needed the work. Some Government Board ordered me to fire the new men now working for me and to rehire the men who had quit, to pay them wages for the time they were striking. This would have cost me thousands of dollars I did not have. I couldn't do this and told the Government man so. He said: "You have a Union mine. You will do as we tell you, or we will take your mine and operate it in the name of the United States."
>
> My lawyer, Mr. Mason, told me they couldn't do this without going into Court, where I could have my day in Court. But on Monday morning, July ———, about daylight, several armed West Virginia State Policemen, one with a machine gun, the others with pistols and rifles, "all loaded", and several men who claimed to be Navy officers—that one sitting there (Fox pointed to Lieutenant Commander ———, who was sitting at the Government counsel table) told me to get off my property. They made me leave my office and took charge of everything, all my supplies, all my records. They then fired my men. They hired in their place the men who had quit and gone on strike. There were

86

also some Union people, the United Mine Union men, there, I
believe the same ones I see now sitting back there in this Court
Room. I had a good mine with plenty of supplies all paid for. I
had been producing about 300 tons of Pittsburgh coal each day.
I was paying my bills and getting along good when they did this
to me. Now, Judge, my mine is ruined. They have broke through
the main heading, and surface water is running into it. It will be
"drowned out" before long.

They have operated it for three months now. They have the
same men I had, who mined 300 tons of coal a day, but now I am
told they don't average 50 tons a day. They have spent thousands of dollars. They brought two men from New York to act
as appraisers. They hired a full time bookkeeper. They have
three Navy officers on the payroll. They have broke me.

You see, Judge, you had me up here once for selling whiskey.
You sent me away and told me never to come back in this Court
again. I have been trying to make an honest living ever since. I
have a wife and a boy. But they have really fixed me now.

Judge Baker: Mr. Fox when I said never come back into this
Court, I didn't mean a case of this sort.

Fox identified the people whom he claimed had forcibly
seized his property, and he asked Judge Baker to return the
same to him.

The Assistant Attorney General from Washington then
cross-examined Mr. Fox for hours. I've never been certain
about what he was trying to ascertain. It was not about the
seizing of the mine, nor about the production of coal, nor the
ownership. He seemed to be more interested in forcing Fox to
comply with the wishes of the coal miners union than he was
with the production of coal, for which the mine was supposedly
seized.

We then produced many witnesses who testified that the
Fox mine, which they had inspected, was being irreparably
damaged, that it was true that a breakthrough to the surface
on the main haulageway had occurred, and water would enter
same and greatly damage the mine.

Lieutenant Commander ——— took the stand as a witness
for the Federal Government. He produced military orders as-
signing him to the Department of Interior for the purpose of
seizing the Fox mine. He stated he secured the aid of the armed

State Police to assist him, because he did not want any violence to occur while he was taking over and operating the coal mine belonging to Fox.

I questioned him as to the number of employees now working at the mine and was surprised to find that 30 people now worked there, not including himself and his three assistants, or a total of 33. He admitted that during the three months the United States Government had operated the mine, fewer than 50 tons of coal per day had been produced. He further admitted that the mine was being operated at a loss and that the Government had expended $145,000 in excess of the money received for the coal sold during the three months it had charge of the mine. This did not include his salary as a Lieutenant Commander, nor the salary of his two brother naval officers.

The representatives of the miners' union were present and testified for the Government to the effect that the eighteen Union miners fired by Fox, as they stated, had been re-employed by the United States Government.

The trial lasted over a period of three weeks, and Fox was forced to spend all the money he had saved or could borrow, to pay the expense of the witnesses, since Wheeling is about eighty miles from Morgantown, and many hotel bills and travel expenses were incurred.

The case was submitted to Judge Baker who had heard all the evidence.

I argued that a great injustice had been done to Fox when his property was seized by force and arms. I reminded the Judge that courts were open to the Government at all times, and if the Government needed the coal production from the Fox mine, a Court proceeding could have secured the same. I stated it seemed to me to be very ridiculous that a mighty government like ours could consider it necessary to national defense to seize a little coal mine producing such a small quantity of coal. I said, "Why the war was over in 1945. Certainly the War Powers Act should not be resorted to by our great Government." I showed the Judge that the act would expire within the next five months.

I stressed the waste being committed by the Government in expending almost $200,000 of the taxpayers' money to seize and operate this mine. I inquired what the reason could be, and I answered the question myself—political; to appease the miners' union and to get the votes and union support. At this remark, the good Judge smiled and said: "Mr. Mason, are you making a legal argument, or a political speech?" I felt we had won our case in this Court and that we rightfully should have. I sat down, and Mr. Hayden, the Assistant U.S. Attorney from Washington, gave his argument.

He continued to assert this Court was without authority to hear the case since it involved the Secretary of Interior, a cabinet officer. Then he moved into the great power of the Government to seize property for national defense purposes. He told the Court about the United States Government seizing the great Montgomery Ward stores about a year ago because they failed to comply with price fixing. He said Mr. Sewell Avery, the President of the Company, was bodily carried from his office by U.S. armed soldiers. The Judge was particularly interested in this, and I knew why; his son-in-law was a Vice-President of this company.

Mr. Hayden seemed to believe that the United States Government could do as it pleased with private property, so long as someone in Washington thought it was needed to aid a wartime economy. He argued long and loud.

His Honor finally said: "Gentlemen, I've heard enough. I've been patient a long time, listened to you for many hours, heard the testimony of many witnesses. I now decide this case.

> In my thirty years as a Judge of this Court, I have never seen a more flagrant abuse of power by agents of this great Government of ours. I said, abuse of power by agents, and not abuse by our Government. It was never intended that men in Government should abuse its citizens. The founding fathers knew of these abuses in England, and that is why the power of men, acting as government agents, was curbed by our Bill of Rights, as the first eight Amendments to our United States Constitution is called.
>
> This government of ours is a government of laws, and not a government of men. Further, gentlemen, no man is above the law, and no man is below the law.
>
> Mr. Fox, I am ordering the Secretary of the Interior, Mr.

89

Krug, to turn over your property to you—now—immediately. You attorneys prepare the order and submit the same to me.

This was Wednesday, February 14, 1954.

It is customary for the attorney prevailing in a legal action to prepare the order of the Judge for signature; to first submit the same to the opposing counsel and have it approved; and then to submit the same to the Judge for his signature and entry; hence the phrase, "the Court speaks only by its orders and decrees." I prepared the order carrying out the Honorable William E. Baker's decision. It was approved by Mr. Hayden, of the Attorney General's office, and presented to the Clerk, a Mr. William Howard, who said he would have Judge Baker enter the same, that the Judge had been called to his hotel.

In Federal United States Courts, an appeal from a District Court to a three-judge Court, designated as the Circuit Court of Appeals, is a matter of right. No opposition can be made of it. Once an appeal is taken, the record, being all of the testimony and orders entered in the lower Court, is printed, and it, together with printed briefs, is submitted to the Circuit Court of Appeals. A time is then fixed for oral argument. The attorneys on both sides appear, argue this case, and submit the same to the Judges. Usually in two or three months thereafter the Judges announce their opinion in writing. In some cases an appeal may be taken from the decision of the Circuit Court of Appeals to the Supreme Court of the United States. Usually such an appeal is only granted in cases involving the construction of some part of the United States Constitution.

I felt certain that the Attorney General of the United States would appeal Judge Baker's decision. However, I was not prepared for what happened. Indeed, I was greatly surprised, for new unusual legal history, to me, at least, was about to be made.

On Thursday, February 16th, two days after Judge Baker's decision, I received a phone call from the Clerk of the United States Circuit Court of Appeals in Richmond, Virginia, advising me that the United States Government wanted to take an appeal from Judge Baker's decision in the District Court, and that the presiding Judge of the Circuit Court of Appeals wanted me to be present in their Court the next morning to discuss the appeal. I politely advised the Clerk that I knew an appeal could be taken in the Fox Case as a matter of right, that there was no reason for me to be present, that I could do nothing to prevent the appeal from being granted, and I would not be there. Within a few minutes my phone again rang, and the Clerk of the Circuit Court of Appeals again identified himself, stating that the Court had ordered me to be present in the Court at Richmond the next morning.

The weather was very bad, but since airplanes were not available in those years in my mountain town of Morgantown, West Virginia, I drove most of the night and was present in the United States Circuit Court Room in Richmond, Virginia, early the next morning when Court convened.

The Court was then composed of three prominent men as Judges: Judge Parker, the President of the Court, had been one of the presiding Judges on the first Nuremberg trials which had tried Goering and other top Nazis; Judge Soper was a very experienced Judge; and Judge Dobie had been Dean of the Law School of the University of Virginia who had written several books on the law. The law set forth in one of these I was to confront him with later in my legal argment in the Fox Case.

When Court convened, and the President had conferred with the Clerk in a whispered conversation, I sensed something was wrong, and then Judge Parker announced Court would recess until 1:30 p.m. I was later to learn that Judge Baker had neglected to sign his order carrying out his decision; so there was nothing to appeal from at that morning session. I later learned that Mr. Howard, the Clerk of the District Court, journeyed to Berkeley Springs, West Virginia, where Judge Baker spent his weekend. He had the good Judge sign the order, and then phoned the Clerk of the Circuit Court of Appeals informing him of the same. Thus when the Court again convened at 1:30 p.m., for the first time this high United States Circuit Court of Appeals could act upon the appeal.

Judge Parker: "Attorney Mason, won't you agree that Judge Baker's order should be abated until this appeal is disposed of?"

Attorney Mason: "No, sir, Your Honor, I have worked long

91

and hard to protect the property rights of my client, and I'm not giving them away now."

Judge Parker: "Very well, the appeal is granted, and the order of the District Judge, William E. Baker, stayed."

Now, indeed, new and novel proceedings were to commence.

Judge Parker: "Gentlemen, when can you be ready to make final argument of the case?"

Attorney Mason: "Why, sir, it will take several months to print the record and briefs."

Judge Parker: "The case may be submitted on a typewritten record, and likewise typewritten briefs. This can be done six weeks from today. We will hear final argument in this case on ——— April, ———.

Now I had indeed witnessed the awesome power and might of the legal branch of this, our Federal Government. Was it possible that men in our Justice Department could contact Federal Judges and cause new procedures to be followed? Judge Baker had said this was a government of laws, and not of men. I wondered. Here was a little individual who had won his case before a Federal Court; but before he received the benefit of the Court's decision, his rights were snatched away in a most unusual manner. Now where were we going?

The record was typewritten. The briefs were typewritten.

We were in the Federal Court Room in that stately city of Richmond, Virginia, again.

The astute Attorney General, Mr. Hayden, had again made his argument to the three-judge Court. I could see he had convinced them that our nation was still at war—in 1951.

I arose to make my argument.

Judge Parker: "Mr. Mason, we want you to answer Mr. Hayden. How do you answer his argument that World War II is not over?"

Mr. Mason: "Your Honor, I think you know it's over because you sat as a Judge in the Nuremberg trials. If you will pardon me, sirs, for being personal, I was in the City of Munich, Germany, on the 8th day of May, 1945, and when the shooting stopped that night I was glad the European War was over."

Judge Dobie: "Mr. Mason, what do you say to Mr. Hayden's argument that the District Court did not have jurisdiction?"

92

Mr. Mason: "Your Honor, I read from Page 107, Paragraph b, Dobie on Injunctions, written by you five years ago, as follows:

" 'Federal District Courts have jurisdiction to grant mandatory injunctions restoring property to their owners against cabinet officers when it is shown irreparable injury or waste is being committed.' Sir, with all due respect, if you reverse this case, you will have to rewrite your book."

The case was over. I knew I had lost. Within a few days a very short opinion was handed down saying the District Court was without jurisdiction, and regardless of same, the War Powers Act gave the Government the authority to seize property as it had in the Fox Case—this though our country had been at peace for five years or more.

If Fox and I could have gone to the Supreme Court of the United States, we would have won our case, because several months thereafter Mr. Truman seized the U.S. Steel Company and the Supreme Court held the seizure was illegal upon the same reasons I had assigned in the Fox Case.

A small businessman, in this "government of laws, and not of men" has little chance of winning in the courts against the government.

What happened to the Fox Coal Company? Shortly after the decision of the Circuit Court of Appeals the Government abandoned the operation of the Fox Coal Company and returned what was left of the property to Ralph Fox.

We later filed a suit in the United States Court of Claims in Washington, D.C. This suit was settled about a year later for a sum of money that in no wise compensated Fox for the damages to his mine.

Why didn't we appeal the decision of the Circuit Court of Appeals to the United States Supreme Court? There were two reasons. When the property was returned to us, there was nothing to appeal from. Secondly, the cost of the same was more than a little businessman like Fox could afford.

What did our great United States Federal Government prove by the Fox Case? Again I wondered—did we have a government of laws, or a government of men—and some of them in the government who were pygmies?

Oscar Reed—'Murder, 1st Degree'

In the middle 1930s I was appointed to defend a colored gentleman named Oscar Reed, who was charged with the murder of a fellow colored man in the village of Osage, a mining community in Monongalia County, West Virginia, about seven miles from Morgantown.

Reed freely admitted the killing which was done with what is now called a "Saturday Night Special." His defenses were self-defense of his home and family which consisted of his wife.

Reed professed to be a very religious man. He claimed that upon many occasions the deceased, whom he had killed, would walk by his house when he was on his knees praying, as he said, "to his God." The deceased would frequently walk by and say, "You better pray, you black son of a bitch, for I'm going to kill you!"

He claimed further that the deceased's conduct toward him continued over a period of years—and in addition to his threats to him, he frequently cursed and abused his wife without any reason.

Reed was a tall, strongly built man. He seemed very polite and pleasant when I was examining him during his trial. Relating in detail the many threats on his life and the conduct of the deceased, the jury seemed sympathetic toward his conduct on the witness stand.

I had completed the details of the deceased's conduct and turned my client over to the prosecuting attorney for cross-examination.

Upon being questioned by the prosecutor, his meek, courteous attitude seemed to change, and he became very antagonistic toward the prosecutor. The prosecutor was inquiring about the name calling and the threats.

I saw we were losing ground with the jury, due, I thought, to my client's belligerent attitude toward the prosecutor. I called for a recess, which the court granted. Then, I consulted with my client. I said, "Do you want to die?" He said, "No." I then said, "If you don't change your attitude toward the prosecutor, the jury may hang you."

The recess being over, the prosecutor continued his cross examination of Reed. His first question was, "You say he called your wife names? What names did he call her?"

Reed burst out crying in a very loud voice and said, "He called my wife a cow." He continued to cry loud and long at each question from the prosecutor thereafter.

After summation had been made, the jury took only a few minutes to find Reed not guilty.

It is my belief that his tears and loud crying did more to acquit him than my argument and the Judge's instructions to the jury upon a man's right to protect his home and castle.

The Case I Won on a Dead Man's Testimony

He was a big, healthy man about fifty years old. He lived in our town—Morgantown, West Virginia. He worked for the U.S. Bureau of Internal Revenue as an assistant to the Chief of the Bureau.

The year was in the late thirties—the month was December. It was a cold, snowy day and he was walking on his way to work. He slipped on the icy street and fell, injuring his back. When his Chief arrived at work, he found him lying on a large table moaning and groaning, and when the Chief inquired of his pain, he stated, "I slipped on the icy street and injured my back."

Within a few weeks he died.

He had purchased an insurance policy that provided double indemnity in case of an injury received in an accident. The insurance company refused to pay on the grounds that his death was not caused by the accident.

His widow, the beneficiary in the policy of insurance, consulted me; and I proceeded to sue the insurance company claiming the cause of death was the injuries received in the fall on the icy street.

The insurance company defended the case in court upon the grounds that the accident did not cause the death; and further that the deceased's statement to his employer about the fall was inadmissible testimony in a court of law upon the ground that it was hearsay testimony; and upon the further ground that there was no evidence that the injuries caused his death.

I produced a reputable doctor who testified that a "trauma," a blow, in his opinion, had produced a blood clot which, in turn, entered his heart causing death—"Coronary Thrombosis."

Now, it was necessary for me to establish an exception to the well-known hearsay rule of evidence.

Much research of the law produced many cases in various states holding that statements made by someone suffering pain and stating the cause of same shortly after an accident, were an exception to the hearsay rule of evidence and were what was known as "Spontaneous Exclamations" and were, therefore, admissible in evidence. The Circuit Court admitted the testimony of the dead man made to his employer, and the jury decided in favor of the widow.

The case was appealed to our Supreme Court which decided for the first time in West Virginia that statements to someone while the injured party was suffering pain were truthworthy and were known as "Spontaneous Exclamations." They were, therefore, admissible in evidence as to what caused the injuries and were an exception to the hearsay rule. Thus, the dead man was allowed to "testify" in Court.

The case will be found in our West Virginia Supreme Court Reports designated as *Collins* vs. *The Equitable Insurance Company*.

The Thirteen Old Men

In the early thirties, during the Great Depression, like most young lawyers, I had very little practice—and in most cases my clients were without money to buy food, much less pay attorney fees.

I was frequently called by some client in our county jail. One morning after having interviewed a client in the jail, as I was leaving I heard someone call my name, "Kermit, come here." The place was what was known as the city range of the jail. The man who called I recognized as an elderly man in his seventies. I knew him. He was a farmer. His name was Lemley.

He said, "Kermit, get me out of here." I said, "Why Mr. Lemley, why are you here?" He said, "My son signed a complaint before the County Clerk charging me with being 'crazy' and they are going to send me to Weston"—which was the place of confinement for insane people. He said, "I'm not crazy; they just want my property and can't wait until I die."

Within a few minutes twelve other elderly men appeared from adjoining cells and told me the same story. Some were crying. All were old men. By looking at them, their knotted hands told of a lifetime of hard work. Some were farmers, some coal miners, some carpenters. I talked to each one, and not one of them appeared to be mentally disturbed.

During this period of time the only thing necessary to commit one to our insane asylum was to have one sign a form before the Clerk of our Court saying the person was insane, and then the Clerk entered an order sending the person to Weston.

Most of these old men had been in the county jail two or three months for the reason that the asylum at Weston was filled up, and there was no room for more patients, "sane or insane."

I was really touched by seeing these elderly people being, in my opinion, illegally detained. I knew the remedy was a writ called a *Habeas Corpus* which meant to produce the body before the Judge of the Court where they were confined.

I carefully prepared the writ and named all responsible parties, including the Governor of the State of West Virginia, the State Board of Control, the Clerk of the County Court, and the person(s) who had signed the complaints, parties to the proceedings.

The case was promptly set for hearings, and within a few days my thirteen clients were back in their homes free men.

This case attracted great publicity. The *Pittsburgh Press,* a large newspaper, sent an investigator to every county in West Virginia. He reported more than one hundred old men were confined the same way.

Our Governor wrote a letter which I still have expressing his apologies and lack of knowledge of the condition of the men.

The results of this case resulted in drastic changes in our

state law. Now no one can be committed to an "Insane Institution" without a full court hearing. The party sought to be committed must be represented by a lawyer and medically examined by a reputable doctor.

Why did an inhuman thing like this happen? A great depression existed at this time. There was no welfare assistance in poor homes; no Social Security; people were hungry; some of the sons testified that they felt their father would be fed and kept better in an institution than in the poverty at home. My belief was that greed entered into the picture too; greed to get control of what dad had worked all his life for. Could this happen today? Hardly, because of the safeguards of our present laws in West Virginia.

Then, too, there is public relief; but the greatest deterrent is Social Security.

When I visit our local banks on "Social Security day," I see many old men, along with their sons and daughters helping dad cash his Social Security check. Now, he is worth keeping at home!

Although I was badly in need of money, I received no fee for this work. However, I got more satisfaction out of it than I did from large fees I sometimes received in much later years.

BOOK THREE

The Political Years

Times Like These Try Men's Souls

*(The Speech I Prepared to Nominate Nelson Rockefeller
for President at the Miami Convention in 1968—
But Did Not Get To Do So)*

Thomas Payne was really concerned about the affairs of this nation when he, though a British-born subject, uttered those often quoted words during the desperate, cold winter at Valley Forge where Washington's cold, sick, barefoot, ragged army was almost losing the Revolutionary War.

Where are they now? The summertime patriots—the sunshine soldiers? Those who survive this and fight on to victory will be remembererd and honored forever by those who love freedom and this nation.

These are not the actual quotes of Mr. Payne's words, but they do, in my opinion, express his thoughts in his writings and speeches in 1775.

How like our present times was our nation then. We were greatly divided. We were in a great Revolutionary War against our mother country. Fear stalked the colonies. The nation was bankrupt. Washington's unpaid army was deserting by the thousands. We had no allies, no credit in the world markets. We were not even a nation—just an English Colony.

One thing we did have, and that was great, courageous leaders—Washington, Jefferson, Adams, Franklin, and lesser known men like Thomas Payne. These men, fearless, proud, but possessed with love of country and for their fellowmen, who created and passed on to their descendants one of the greatest nations that has ever existed in the world. They established for us a government that has withstood many wars, both within the nation and abroad.

A great storehouse of knowledge and material wealth has been created in our country and within the world. Men and women talk, see, and travel in a few hours to almost any spot in the world. The radio, television, and the airplane have really made the "One World" that Wendell Willkie wrote about. Yet with all our strength, knowledge, and wealth, we have not

101

learned to live together in the world. No, we have not even learned to live together in our United States of America.

Murder, assassinations, robbing, burning homes and cities have become the order of the day. We spend billions of dollars for war in the guise of freedom for strange lands, and destroy the homes of helpless people who, until we bombed them, had never heard of our great country. We see on television, or in our travels, our own citizens living in cold, desolate shacks, without the very necessities of life, and we sit in our comfortable homes watching our favorite TV programs, warmed by our gas or electric furnaces, or cooled by an air conditioner, and hear our political leaders say, "You never had it so good."

Your nation's capital burns—fires set by rioters and looters. Your hungry, poor people march to your nation's home in Washington, D.C.; makeshift houses are built for them, and they are allowed to wallow in the mud for a few days. Then their leaders are jailed, because with all the nation's knowledge, power, and wealth, man still fails to communicate with his fellowmen. With all the television coverage available, with radios, advances in electronics, with colleges and institutions of higher learning, with all the forms of communication devised by modern science, man has failed in learning to live together with his fellowman.

I think of the ancient philosophers, the teachers, the writings of the sages, and of the ancient proverb, "Knowledge is the principal thing. Therefore, get knowledge. But with all the getting, get understanding."

I walk the streets of my mountain village, and meet my friend that I have known all my lifetime. Today he does not greet me with a smile, a laugh, and a hearty hail; rather a tear, and in a broken voice he tells me that he just received a telegram from the War Department. His only grandson has been killed in Vietnam.

He says, "I thought we fought World War One to make the world safe for democracy." And then he said to me, "You and I fought in Africa, Italy, France, and Germany, and our comrades fought and died by the thousands in the Pacific theater in the war, the war we were told and believed was to be the 'war to end all wars.' You and I," he said, "had sons fighting in Korea, and now my only grandson has been killed in a war way off in Asia. Remember how Eisenhower said we should never become involved in a land war in Asia; and if I remember correctly, President Johnson said, 'I will never send American boys to die in a war in Asia.' " I said, "You remember correctly." I shook hands with my sad friend and neighbor, and went on my way. But I kept thinking, "What is wrong? Where have we failed?" Then I said to myself, "I know we are wrong." This destruction within and without America must stop. There is something wrong in the logic and thinking of the leaders in America. There must be a change.

Indeed, times like these do try men's souls! This great Republican political party was once the leading party of this nation. It was founded by the immortal Lincoln, nurtured by Teddy Roosevelt, strengthened by Taft, and then uplifted by Eisenhower, the great, admirable war hero. Our Republican party built this nation from a struggling, war-destroyed country in 1865 to one of the proudest, most respected, and one of the wealthiest nations in the world.

Then the Great Depression not only destroyed our political party, but almost destroyed our nation. Let's briefly look over that period of our country's history and the Republican party. In 1932 Hoover was defeated; in 1936 Landon was defeated. In 1940 a young man named Thomas Dewey sought the presidency. He was defeated for the nomination by a former Democrat by the name of Wendell Willkie; Willkie was defeated by Roosevelt. In 1944 Dewey tried again to defeat the Democrat, Truman. Again our party lost. Then came the great Eisenhower, famous for his war exploits, and lo, after many years, the Republican party again led this nation. And then what? The great debate, Nixon vs. Kennedy. Nixon loses. Next, Nixon loses as the candidate for the governorship of his home state of California. Again, he cries, "foul," and says he is through; and blames the press and all his friends for his loss, and sadly states he will never do it again.

Then out of the Far West comes Goldwater. He will unite our great Republican party. He does to the extent that we, who have spent most of our lives working for the Republican party have become tired of the system, of the political professionals

103

stacking the Republican National Conventions, as they have done for thirty years, nominating their choices instead of the choices of the American people.

The Republican party used to be the party of the common people. It was in Lincoln's and Grant's day. It was for a short period under the great Eisenhower. It was also said to have been the party of peace. If we look backward forty years, any schoolboy can tell you the political party that has involved this nation in war was the Democratic party.

I have attended four National Conventions, three as a delegate, and one as a spectator, and will say that in each, the delegates did not nominate the choice of the people for president and vice-president. I say this even though President Eisenhower was the choice in one of the conventions. He was indeed the choice of the people, but he was pressured into accepting Nixon for vice-president, when, in my opinion, the people in 1960 did not want Nixon.

In 1968 we meet again, this time in Miami. What do we have? A candidate of the professionals! A man that President Eisenhower thought of dumping in his first campaign because of what some considered dishonesty over accepting money while a United States Senator. A man who was defeated by the choice of the American electorate, young Mr. Kennedy. A man who was defeated for Governor of California. A man who, for eight years as vice-president, never raised his voice to aid the poor. A man who was not then disturbed by the crime in Washington. A man who one day says he has a plan to end the war in Vietnam, and says the next that the war in Vietnam must be won.

Where are the men of vision in America today? There used to be young men of vision: Jefferson, at age thirty-one wrote the Declaration of Independence, Washington was twenty-one when he built Fort Necessity, Patrick Henry was twenty-seven when he said in a stirring speech in the Virginia Assembly, "Give me liberty, or give me death!"

Are there none today in America as proven leaders? Yes, my friends, there are. There are still men of vision, men who have won political campaigns, men admired and respected as world leaders. There are such men in the Republican party, though

104

it is only a minority party. To win an election, it must nominate a man that will appeal not only to Republicans, but to Democrats and Independents as well, but most importantly, to the youth of America. That man is Nelson Rockefeller.

The 1940 Republican Nominating Convention

This is November 1970. Thirty years ago I was considerably younger and very new in politics.

I was a registered Republican. My father and mother were Republicans, as were my grandparents. I was not too sure why, but then I knew that Grandfather had been a sergeant in Company A of the famed Seventh West Virginia regiment and had fought with many generals in the Civil War from Romney to Appomattox; that Abe Lincoln had, during that war, divided Virginia and made our mountains a separate state, and that after that war, Lincoln had given his veterans liberal pensions.

I also knew that when Grant had become president he had appointed my grandfather, who had been a Civil War veteran, postmaster of the village where I was born and had lived all of my early life, thus making him a very distinguished and independent citizen in that town.

In 1940 there were still supposed to be considerable differences between the two great political parties. The Republican party was spoken of as the Party of Peace. We remembered how Wilson had run on a platform of peace with the slogan, "He kept us out of war!"; and then very shortly after got us into World War I.

There had been some talk that our Grand Old Party of Republicans stood for something like a protective tariff, and that the Democratic party stood for something like free trade. I believed then that there was a great difference between those two parties. I was proud to be a Republican.

I was so proud that I entered my name in the 1940 primary election on the Republican ticket as a delegate to the 1940 Republican National Convention, and, somewhat to my surprise, was elected as one of the two delegates from what was then the sixteenth county district of West Virginia.

Shortly after the election I began to receive letters, pamphlets, and even books written about the lives of the candidates for President. However, my mind was made up. As a lawyer, I was a great admirer of Thomas E. Dewey, the then great gang buster District Attorney of New York City.

About a month before the convention we met in our capital city of Charleston, West Virginia, in a party caucus, and organized our West Virginia Delegation which, as I recall, consisted of twenty-three elected delegates.

Mr. Dewey appeared at our caucus. It was the first time I had seen him. He was young, vigorous, "fiery," and fine looking. He spoke to us about his campaigning, conducted then by train. He told us about his humble farmhouse in the state of New York and about his family. He talked about how he could, and would, if nominated, defeat Mr. Roosevelt. I had already been sold on him—now I was really fascinated.

The great day soon came, and we from West Virginia assembled with hundreds of other delegates and political people in the great city of Philadelphia. The leader of our West Virginia delegates was a distinguished citizen, Walter Hallihan. He was supposed to have become very wealthy from Texas oil. For years he had reputedly slated and financed delegates to party conventions in West Virginia. Though I had not been on Walter's slate, he did not pressure or attempt to influence me. I later got to know Walter better from much more political activity on my part, and must say I regarded him as a very fine, upright leader of our party. Politics were a very necessary part of his life, and he loved it. He was very highly regarded in the higher echelon of the Republican party.

I had not been in the City of Brotherly Love for very long before I realized there was more than one candidate for our party's highest honor, the nominee for President of the United States. There was Senator Robert Taft, the Senator from Ohio. Mr. Taft's headquarters consisted of a whole floor of the large Ben Franklin Hotel. Soon I was invited and escorted into the Senator's presence and introduced to him and his wife. I was presented with a souvenir of the convention by Mrs. Taft,

106

which consisted of a diary. I still have it, though I never made an entry in it. This is probably one of the reasons that my wife still lives with me!

I remember Senator Taft as a very tall, formal, distinguished man, and his wife as a very friendly person with an excellent personality. I thought she would have been a good person to be a candidate for office. I was impressed with Senator Taft; however, my man was still Dewey.

There was Senator Vandenberg from Michigan, also a candidate for President of the United States. His headquarters were in the Adelphia Hotel. He was a very distinguished man, and I was greatly impressed with him. I was somewhat taken back, though, to see the crowded bar at his reception on a Sunday afternoon, where many of the delegates had too much to drink.

My neighboring state of Pennsylvania also had a candidate for President, Governor James. I visited him but came away still for Dewey.

There was a very wealthy man, a very powerful newspaper owner named Frank Gannett, from Rochester, New York, who also aspired for the top position. He also had a whole floor of the Ben Franklin Hotel. He had imported live elephants to Philadelphia. His wealth and his power over the press did not impress many of the delegates since, as I remember, he did not get very far.

Not very long after being elected a delegate, I received a letter from a man by the name of Oren Root of New York State telling me what a fine candidate whom I had never then heard of, one Wendell Willkie, would make for President.

On Saturday before the convention was to convene, proudly wearing my delegate's badge, I was often accosted by young people telling me of the great qualities of Willkie, and what a fine candidate for President he would be. Early on Sunday morning, I decided to visit Willkie's headquarters. I found them on the top floor of the Ben Franklin Hotel. Instead of consisting of a whole floor, with many attendants scurrying around, like most of the other political headquarters, I found only a small parlor suite at the end of the hallway. He alone was present. Seeing my delegate's badge as he greeted me in

107

the doorway, he grabbed my hand with a firm grip and invited me to sit down.

Wendell Willkie was a man then in his prime, possibly nearing fifty. He was large and very distinguished looking. I knew he was a lawyer. We discussed the law and politics for a few moments. Then the subject of the approaching war came up. I told him I was afraid that President Roosevelt was going to get us into the European war. I said to him, "Roosevelt is constantly criticizing Germany, it's like me going out on my front porch and threatening my neighbor—soon he has to come out and fight me." He replied, "If I'm elected President, I'll keep this country out of war."

We talked for a long time, and after I arose to leave he said, "Mason, I'm going to be the nominee, you had better get on my bandwagon." I thanked him, told him I was pledged to Dewey and departed, thinking Mr. Willkie was a nice man, but that he had little chance of ever being the Republican nominee for President.

The Convention opened Monday morning and continued for the next five days. The keynote speaker, the principal speaker opening a convention, was a fine looking, very young man, Governor of Minnesota, Harold Stassen. Mr. Stassen had been elected Governor of Minnesota shortly after he was graduated from law school. He was an imposing figure of a man and his position and youth gave him much glamor. He made a rousing, patriotic speech which set the convention off in high spirits.

There was no air-conditioning in 1940 and the Klieg lights made the convention hall very hot. Remember too, that there was no television in 1940—nothing but the movie camera and the radio. It was noticeable from the beginning that the galleries were filled with good-looking young people of both sexes, and it later became apparent that most of them were Willkie supporters. Frequently one would hear them shout, "We want Willkie!"

In 1940, candidates for President still came to the convention city, and although they did not personally, at the beginning, appear at the convention, they, through their workers, did give special attention to the delegates. Being for Dewey, I was frequently invited to his quarters where I met his beautiful wife.

She was an excellent, gracious person and was great reason, I'm sure, for Mr. Dewey's success in both his legal profession and his political life.

One of the most interesting, fascinating women I was to meet at the Dewey headquarters was Mrs. Alice Roosevelt Longworth. She is the daughter of that great man, once one of our most famous Republican presidents, Teddy Roosevelt. When I was introduced to her, I commented, "What is one with a Roosevelt name doing at a Republican Convention?" "I'm one of the out-of-season Roosevelts from Oyster Bay!" she glibly replied. I had many, many very interesting talks with her thirty years ago about her great father and family. I noticed that in the November 1970 issue of *Time* that she was mentioned as still "ruling" the roost of Washington top society.

The platform of the Republicans was presented to the Convention, containing the usual bad things that the Democratic party had been doing and the usual great promises the Republican party would do if it returned to power. Then the great speechmaking commenced and went on for most of three days. Taft, Dewey, James, Gannett, Vandenberg, Willkie and possibly one or two more were finally nominated for President. During all of the speeches, the youths in the galleries constantly screamed over and over for Willkie. It was a constant chant—I can almost hear it forty-five years later—"We want Willkie!"

The great Joseph Martin, the longtime Congressman from Massachusetts, was the Chairman of the Convention. I don't think a fairer man could have presided, yet many times he had to appeal to the people in the galleries to be fair and let the speakers on the platform be heard, asking them to refrain from their shouts while the nominating speeches of other candidates were being made.

Then finally came the balloting. My favorite candidate Tom Dewey led, but in such a large field of candidates, he soon began to lose some of his support. As ballot after ballot continued, Willkie gained until, I believe, on the seventh round, he was nominated for President of the United States.

It was almost over, this unusual Convention of 1940. The next day someone was nominated for Vice-President. There were very few delegates present at that session, and I thought almost anyone would have got more support than McNary of Oregon, as I believe the nominee was.

Many old party workers seemed surprised and stunned that Willkie was nominated by our Republican party. Many said, "How could this happen, how could this unknown man, for many years a registered Democrat, be nominated for President on the Republican ticket?" I've never been too sure. I've been told the seats in the large gallery, which were for non-delegates, had been filled on forged tickets by Willkie supporters. I do know that it was almost impossible for a Republican delegate to get a ticket for any of his friends in the gallery.

Looking back forty-five years, I believe the organization of Willkie and Oren Root, the selection of hundreds of good-looking young people constantly chanting, "We want Willkie," almost hypnotized the delegates.

Shortly before the balloting was to commence I had received many telegrams from prominent people all over West Virginia, reading "Support Willkie." These appear to have been sponsored by Mr. Willkie's organization since most of the delegates received the same "form" telegrams. They were very effective since they allegedly came from many leading citizens.

History has recorded what the results were. Willkie campaigned hard, but after a few speeches, became hoarse and almost lost his voice. Franklin D. Roosevelt badly defeated him, but graciously appointed him to make a world tour, which Willkie did, returning to write a book entitled, *One World.* It was an interesting description of his trip, and told how the new air travel had brought this world much closer together, making the planet "one world." He sent me an autographed copy of it which I now have in my home library.

I was to see Mr. Willkie again when he visited San Antonio, Texas, in 1943. I was stationed there in the United States Army during World War II. I talked with him in the Baker Hotel. I believe he was probably thinking of trying to again get the nomination for the next Presidential election since he introduced me to some of the party leaders from Texas. I never saw him again and, as I recall, he died a year or so later. My friend

Tom Dewey was to receive our Party's nomination twice thereafter, only to be defeated.

Another man that I admired and respected at that convention was to die leading his troops during the Normandy invasion of France in that war that Mr. Willkie said he would prevent: Teddy Roosevelt, Jr., the half-brother of that gracious lady. Alice Roosevelt Longworth. Also present, though only sixteen years of age was a young man frequently mentioned as a good prospect for President during the 1968 Miami convention. He became the mayor of the great city of New York. His name was John Lindsay.

I have attended most of our Republican conventions since 1940—but there has never been one since so full of excitement and surprise.

Nixon, the Vice Presidency, and Wheeling, West Virginia

It was autumn 1952—

The great General Eisenhower, who had directed the greatest crusade known to so-called civilized men, the battle to defeat the dictators of continental Europe—Hitler and Mussolini—had reluctantly agreed to accept his Party's nomination for President of our United States and was holding a great political rally in Wheeling, West Virginia.

The nominee for Vice-President, along with the great illustrious Eisenhower, was a young United States Senator, then serving his first term in the Senate from the state of California. He was first a Congressman from his district in that state, and had received national publicity when he had successfully prosecuted a prominent man in our State Department named Alger Hiss for giving government secrets to Communist agents. The trial of the Hiss case had brought out information that greatly startled the American public. Hiss was a graduate of Harvard. His position in the State Department had brought him in contact with President Franklin D. Roosevelt. He had been Roosevelt's close advisor at the Yalta Conference with the Russians

111

and our other allies, held before World War II ended. It had greatly shaped the future of our relations with Soviet Russia. Alger Hiss was convicted and sentenced to prison due to the efforts of Richard Nixon, member of Congress, and Hiss's name was despised along with that of other traitors to our nation.

President Truman claimed the case was political. He called it a "Red Herring" and the Secretary of State, Dean Acheson, said, "I'll never turn my back on Alger Hiss." As these great political issues came into being, Congressman Nixon was elected to the great august body—the United States Senate. Now he was the choice of his party and had been nominated for Vice-President of the United States to run along with General Dwight Eisenhower. Then there was an explosion—a political explosion.

The press printed a story claiming that Senator Nixon had been receiving a secret fund of money paid to him by a group of his political supporters in California. This story hit every newsstand in the country. Editors wrote editorials. Columnists wrote, and rewrote, their opinions.

The Republican party had not won a national election for twenty long years, and now it seemed their hopes were gone. If the story continued to spread, it would defeat the party and cause Eisenhower to be defeated—such was the belief of many of the Party's leaders. Immediately, many of them urged Eisenhower to dump Nixon—telling him that unless he did so, he would be defeated in the election. However, the great General was not to be pressured into quick action—he had learned, and knew about, the value of loyalty. Men who had fought wars and been close to death, under fire of shot and shell, were always considerate of their fellow "comrades." Eisenhower contacted Nixon and suggested he make a statement to the public, after which the General would decide what action to take.

Senator Richard Nixon announced that on a specified date he would make a nationwide radio speech, telling the American people about the so-called secret fund. The speech was made—it electrified the nation. People who heard it on the radio applauded, whistled, and yelled. Those who read it cried and reread it. It was a great speech. It was approved by the Repub-

lican officials in charge of the campaign funds and was re-
broadcasted many times.

The speech outlined the life of a young man born to a poor
family; the usual, common, poor American family—poor in
money but rich in the American heritage that one must con-
tinually seek something better for their children. There was
talk of a great mother, a Christian mother, ambitious like all
American mothers for the best for her children. It told of the
early struggle in a small California town; of a father devout
and honest who struggled to fight off disaster in the operation
of a small grocery store in those awful days of the Great Depression in the 1930s.

The school days were mentioned—the scholarship, the attempt to play football and the failure to make the team, the
graduation from college, law school, the small law practice—
not much profit. The great war came and with it his struggle
over whether to join up due to his respect for his Quaker
mother, who was so much against war.

The speech told of his enlistment and service to his country—of a beautiful woman named Pat who came into his life,
his courtship and marriage and the babies (two girls). Then the
political battles were told—Congress, his fight against Communists, his election to the Senate and of the great expenses
which he could not meet, and of the loyal friends in California
coming to his aid.

He gave a complete inventory of the fund, which was not
very large. He told of his and Pat's small funds—her thread-
bare coat—of the children's dog.

The speech was a masterpiece. Those who heard it responded by sending thousands of telegrams to General Eisenhower, praising Nixon and urging that he be retained on the
Republican ticket as Vice-President. Nixon was in California.
Eisenhower was in Ohio at a political meeting. He wired Nixon
to meet him in Wheeling, West Virginia, the next evening
where he was to attend a Republican rally. In those days of
1952, the jet airplane was unknown. The trip from California to
West Virginia was slow and tedious.

In 1952, the announcement that the great General Eisenhower would be present any place in the U.S.A. was sufficient

113

in itself to draw a huge crowd. He was not only admired by the American public, but he was their hero too. Many young soldiers who had served under his command in the European theatre wanted again to see their great commander. In addition to his popularity, Eisenhower had announced that he would make a major political address in Wheeling, West Virginia, where he would be joined by his Vice-Presidential candidate, Richard Nixon. At that time, he would announce his decision as to whether or not Nixon would continue on the ticket.

There was a huge crowd assembled. However, the speakers were delayed after it was announced that Nixon's plane was late. The bands played. The local candidates were encouraged to make lengthy speeches. The crowd grew listless, but waited for what lengthened into hours. It was almost 11:00 P.M. when a loud applause issued from the huge crowd as Eisenhower arrived with Senator Nixon. The great General raised his hands skyward, raising Nixon's along with his. I thought I heard the General say to Nixon, "Son, I'm proud of you—you're my boy." The crowd yelled, screamed, and stomped their approval; for then it was known that Nixon was and would continue as the candidate along with General Eisenhower.

Nixon was then introduced to the large gathering. General Eisenhower commenced his speech. Nixon retreated into the background of the large platform.

There on that platform were many of the leaders of the government: Senator Carlson of Kansas; Senator Mundt of South Dakota; Walter Hallen; Rush D. Holt, a former Senator of West Virginia and the candidate for Governor of that state; the Senatoral nominee on the Republican ticket for the U.S. Senate from West Virginia, Chapman Revercomb; and many others. I was the Republican nominee for Congress from the West Virginia Second Congressional District and thus I was invited to sit on the platform.

Senator Nixon took a seat in a remote corner of the platform. I saw him cover his face with his hands and saw the tears travel down his cheeks. He then restrained himself and sat quietly through the proceedings.

The speeches ended, and the crowd melted away. Later that evening I met Senator Nixon in the lobby of the McClure Hotel

114

in Wheeling, West Virginia. I introduced myself to him. He held my hand, looked into my eyes and, in a most sincere way said, "Mason, I hope you win and are elected to Congress." I was not elected to Congress, but Dwight Eisenhower and Nixon were elected—President and Vice-President.

Looking back, I wonder what changes in history would have been written had Eisenhower not been the kindly, considerate gentleman that he was. I wonder too how Nixon "kept his cool" as he did in those hectic days of the 1952 campaign when his world must have been close to the brink of disaster. Was this premonition merely a hinge of fate? And was it already pointing in the direction of the Watergate crisis?

An Embarrassing Event at Martinsburg

In the year 1952, as previously stated, I was the Republican nominee for the U.S. Congress from the Second Congressional District of West Virginia, the first year the great, distinguished General Eisenhower ran for President of the United States.

All candidates for major offices were invited to meet in the West Virginia city of Wheeling and to board Eisenhower's special train which ran from Wheeling to Martinsburg, a distance of more than 150 miles.

The train left Wheeling about midnight and arrived in Martinsburg the next afternoon, stopping at several cities such as Keyser, Cumberland and elsewhere along the way. We, of course, had been presented to the great man and had stood with him at the whistle stops where amazingly large crowds of people were always present.

The train ending in Martinsburg, a speakers' platform had been erected there, and the candidates were seated on it. General Eisenhower was the first to be introduced and the first to speak to the large audience. Then, each of the candidates was introduced and invited to say a few words to the large crowd. I was handed a microphone which was near the corner of the platform.

This was a high spot for me—a great moment in my life, and I was attempting to make the most of it.

I learned from a distinguished senator friend, after the rally had ended, thank goodness, that all during my speech I had been standing on, and sometimes stomping the great General's fedora hat, which he had carefully placed in the corner of the platform.

General Eisenhower moaned to my senator friend, "Oh, my God, he's standing on my hat!" He was too much of a gentleman to call it to my attention at the time, and I have always been thankful!

Joe Smith for Vice-President

Joe Smith's name was presented for nomination for Vice-President of United States in 1956. Many thousands of people who were interested in the Republican party and political conventions were greatly surprised, while listening to their radios and televisions, to hear that a new name had arrived on the political scene. Who was Joe Smith and how had he gotten his name before the Republican National Convention?

Harold Stassen, the former youthful governor of Minnesota, was not happy with the then Vice-President Nixon and had started a movement to prevent his nomination for re-election with President Eisenhower, who was certain to be a nominee for a second term as President. Mr. Stassen had contacted many delegates and urged them to write letters to President Eisenhower, requesting him to replace Nixon for a second term as Vice-President.

He presented his favorable delegates with a form letter and designated the place and manner of addressing and mailing the letters. Mr. Stassen had considerable support for what he termed an open convention for the nominee of Vice-President.

Among the candidates most frequently mentioned was Christian Herter, a former governor of a southern state and a very prominent and well-known man. He, it was believed, would greatly strengthen Eisenhower's ticket.

President Eisenhower arrived in San Francisco and received

a great welcome. The Convention unanimously nominated him for re-election as the party's choice for four more years as President of the United States. It soon became apparent to most of the delegates, who had previously favored an open convention, that President Eisenhower wanted to retain Vice-President Nixon for that position to his new four-year term. Most of the delegates acceded to the wishes of President Eisenhower, but not Mr. Stassen, nor one of his followers from Nebraska, a man by the name of Terry Carpenter.

The great distinguished Chairman of that convention was Joseph Martin, a member of Congress for many years. He had been Chairman of many previous Republican Conventions, and a fairer man never presided over a political meeting.

Mr. Carpenter had secured time for his nominating speech, and he, acting for Mr. Stassen and his supporters, was going to nominate Christian Herter instead of Nixon as Vice-President. Joe Martin and the Eisenhower/Nixon supporters knew this, and they persuaded Christian Herter not to allow his name to be presented to the convention as a candidate for the office of Vice-President. Apparently Stassen and his delegate, Terry Carpenter, did not then know this. Mr. Carpenter was entitled to make his speech, and he commenced, resorting to the age old tactics then in use at such gatherings, extolling the virtues of his man, saying over and over, "The man I am about to nominate was governor of a great state, a great statesman and a mighty force for good . . ." etc., etc. Joe Martin kept saying to him in low tones, "Name your man." Mr. Carpenter stuck to his well-prepared speech until his time was almost up. When he was bound to name his man, Christian Herter, Joe Martin placed in front of him on the podium, in bold script, the handwritten letter of Christian Herter, saying, "Under no circumstances will I permit my name to be presented to this convention as a candidate for Vice-President."

Terry Carpenter read the letter, his face flushing. "I said, name your man," Martin continued. Terry Carpenter yelled, "Joe Smith." Joe Smith's name was not voted on by the convention since no one seconded his nomination. It was not very surprising, considering that Joe Smith had not existed during that convention!

117

It May Interest You (May 15, 1964)

The following is an excerpt from the column with this title in the *Dominion-News*, Friday morning, May 15, 1964, written by Bill Hart, Editor, in which as was customary, he refers to himself as z-1:

... there emerged from Tuesday's election (Republican Primary for nomination for President) two "strong men"—rather one s.m. proved beyond the shadow of a doubt he is a "king-maker" as z-1 said he was in 1960 only to be scoffed at by some of the "brethren in the political vineyard" but the second "strong man" came to "command" on Tuesday on the sweep of his man's sensational victory; and about these two men each from a different party z-1 wishes to speak this morning ... let us talk about the second rather than the first for a few moments, shall we? ... z-1 has specific reference to Kermit the first of the House of Mason—otherwise previously to this anointment to political fame and fortune, Kermit Mason, Republican, attorney, real estate tycoon and once upon a time a barefoot boy in the then dusty streets of Albright.

... no other person in West Virginia approaches Senor Mason when it comes to giving credit where credit belongs in the "sensational" victory of Nelson Rockefeller at the polls in the Republican primary in the balloting on Tuesday. ... West Virginia is and was ripe for Rockefeller in 1964 just as it was for Jack Kennedy in 1960 because both have the same basic appeal to West Virginians ... z-1 said publicly and privately Rockefeller would do well—very, very well—here and in West Virginia because he is taking the trouble to go to the "little communities" as well as the big and because his campaign is not based or pitched on the same "no one is right but me" theme that Barry Goldwater has staked his fame and fortune.

... long, long before Rockefeller's appearance in West Virginia the local Republican tycoon was bombarding the New Yorker with messages that West Virginia was fertile ground—that it could begin a groundswell for him just as it had for Kennedy ... the only trouble with Rockefeller he couldn't get anybody—say Goldwater—to get into the race here ... had he his victory would have been much more impressive ... all of these things this guy who needs money like Carter needs more liver pills—Mason—sensed or deducted—any rate he went on that at-

118

tack and all we have to say to him as a fellow Prestonian: get on your horse and go see Rockefeller at once; don't let some johnny-after-the-battle spend a few dollars and hover around Rocky like one person z-1 knows in the Kennedy deal . . . in other words, if Mason lets this golden opportunity slip to become a major kingmaker he isn't as smart as z-1 thinks he is.

The West Virginia Builder

The year was one of the Great Depression years of the early 1930s. The local Court House room was crowded with people. They occupied the jury box, all the seats in the large court room. They were standing in the hallways, along the sides of the benches, occupying the steps leading to the Judge's bench, in the doorways leading into this large room—and many had been turned away hours before the scheduled political meeting was billed to commence.

The people present represented a cross section of Monongalia County, West Virginia. They were unemployed coal miners, unemployed carpenters, bricklayers, painters, laborers, and farmers who were losing their farms to mortgage companies because they could not sell their farm products, although many other people in the county were putting their children to bed hungry and were unable to sleep because they, too, were hungry and cold and worried since they had no income. No jobs, and no future help was in sight.

There were no welfare agencies of the Federal Government, no Unemployment Compensation, no Social Security, no Medicare in that year of 1932. The only agency for help was the County Court, with a very meager tax income not sufficient even to operate a so-called poor house where the aged were sent.

The audience waited eagerly for the political speaker. They were hopeful. They needed help in their miserable condition. There was a sudden hush in the crowded courtroom. Room was made for the entrance of the speaker. He made his way to the Judge's desk and was introduced by a local leader.

He was a very young man of twenty-nine years and very

119

handsome. He bowed to the immense crowd, thanked his introducer, and then, as his first act, he introduced his mother. She was then a greying, middle-aged lady. Then he commenced to speak. He had a marvelous soothing voice. His pronunciation was flawless. He was a trained, talented public speaker. He was making a political speech, since he was the candidate for Congress from the Second Congressional District of West Virginia on the Democratic ticket. He discussed the failure of the Republican party during its past administrations, particularly during the Hoover and Harding administrations. He spoke of a brighter future under the banner of the Democratic party with a leader then little-known in our county by the name of Franklin D. Roosevelt. He spoke of the richness and plenty of a great country filled with abundance for all, yet with a government that was callous enough to allow its people to starve for something to eat, and to die in misery for lack of hospitals and medical attention. The audience cheered, yelled, stomped, and cheered again their approval of his statements.

He carried his campaign through the then eighteen counties of the Congressional District and was elected along with Franklin D. Roosevelt, with the greatest majority that any one had ever received in West Virginia political history. Now he was in a position to keep his promises. He did! He helped get through the Congress of the United States legislation that permitted the leaders of this great, rich, bountiful country to aid its citizens. Soon thousands were employed—on the roads, in the forests, building airports, homes, new towns, colleges, town halls and hospitals. He was elected time after time to Congress.

He did not forget his friends. He had few enemies, and regardless of one's political affiliation his office door was open; and he was willing and able to aid them at all times—and he did.

He served in Congress in his district, the Second Congressional District of West Virginia, for fourteen years with honor and distinction. During his terms World War II commenced and ended. The district became very prosperous, and as people do, they forgot him and he was defeated for his seat in Congress by a returning war hero.

I recall some of the things he helped to accomplish in our Mountain State, and in our great nation:

120

A great welfare program was commenced.

Social Security was enacted.

Unemployment insurance was begun.

Schools were improved.

Airports and roads were built.

A nation won a great worldwide war.

He sponsored and helped pass federal legislation that helped thousands of veterans of the war to secure an education under a so-called G.I. rights bill, and to build their homes and to become good citizens.

He was a great lover of aviation, and helped build fine airports in many sections of our Mountain State and elsewhere in our nation.

He helped start the first transportation of mail by the airplane.

Though defeated for his seat in Congress in 1946, he accepted it graciously and without bitterness, and became employed by an aviation company. He frequently returned to campaign for other members of his party in his forceful manner—in our State, in his old congressional district, and elsewhere.

Then, in a few years, a vacancy occurred in a senatorial seat in Congress in West Virginia. He ran for the seat and was elected to the U.S. Senate. He was now in a position to really aid our state and our nation. Now he could draw upon the many years of knowledge he had gained in Congress and the business world. He used this knowledge wisely and unselfishly. He sponsored and succeeded (almost by himself due to his energy and persuasive powers) in getting the Appalachian Highway Bill passed, which enabled states with small taxing powers to build the so-called interstate highways.

Becoming a member of the most important committees in the great U.S. Senate, he helped build dams for great power projects in our state and nation. Highways—four-lane, magnificent stretches of interstate, are opening vast areas of beautiful West Virginia to tourists and businesses of all kinds. People who had lost hope are now employed—retired people are leading lives of leisure and enjoying their Social Security benefits in Florida and elsewhere. Hospitals and great universities are being built in West Virginia. No longer are children and old people cold and hungry. No longer do the aged walk the streets in despair.

He served in the House of Representatives under Franklin D. Roosevelt during his term as President, then under President Truman. He was regarded by these men as a great leader.

As a United States Senator he and President Johnson worked closely together accomplishing much for the nation and with great benefits for West Virginia. Now, in 1970, President Nixon, a Republican, is in office. Senator Jennings Randolph works, as usual, with him for the good of the nation and his mountain people in West Virginia.

He long ago learned the greatest art of mankind—that of getting along with his fellowmen, getting and maintaining their confidence and self-respect.

Senator Jennings Randolph has kept his promises made in the old Court Room in Morgantown, West Virginia, in 1932— that he would give the people of his state a better and finer life. He has been a builder, not only of bridges, roads, airports, schools and universities, but a builder of character, self-respect and happiness of the people of his Mountain State of West Virginia.

BOOK FOUR

Miscellaneous Personal Recollections

A Westward Journey, 1924

It was June 1924—

I was the proud possessor of a 1923 Model 490 Chevrolet. It was an automobile that the young General Motors Company was building in Flint, Michigan, to compete with Henry Ford's Model T. It sold for around the same vast sum of $350.

The 490 was a "Touring Car" which meant that it had no glass windows like a modern sedan, but possessed a top and, when it rained, side curtains were available, providing one could withstand the struggle of getting them on. It may have had a self-starter, but as I remember, it seldom worked and, if it did not, there was always the "muscle-powered" crank. With its four cylinders wide open on a good road (if such could be found) one could frighten the horses and chickens for miles around at the astounding speed of forty miles per hour! This, of course, required a young and reckless driver with a burning desire to risk his life. It had no power steering, no automatic gears and, unless the driver was a master of the clutch, the car would leap forward like a bucking bronco when gears were shifted. Unlike the Model T, with its three foot pedals, it had a gear shift "on the floor," along with a "foot-feed" (accelerator).

Before the three of us departed on our long planned trip West, we made some necessary purchases with what little money we had. We bought an "automobile tent," a gasoline stove, a gasoline-burning lantern, three canvas folding cots and some cooking utensils. We borrowed some blankets from home and, armed with a map of the United States, we set out on our adventure.

The three of us were myself, then twenty-one, a college student who had never traveled farther than from Albrightsville, West Virginia, to Morgantown, a distance, as the Chevy chugs, of about twenty-five miles; "Tater," a Rembrandt of a sign painter; and "Bill" who painted houses.

The Great Day arrived! We left Morgantown with our car loaded down with camping gear and headed westward toward Wheeling, West Virginia. Our journey took us to Route 40,

"The National Pike," the famous western highway which ran from Cumberland, Maryland, to Vandalia, Illinois.

Kicking up a wide trail of dust by our reckless driving, we arrived at Bellaire, Ohio, a few miles west of Wheeling, where we stopped and camped for the night.

Sleeping that night was poor as we had not yet learned to sleep with equal parts of the blanket under us and on top. When daylight came, I, the designated cook, fired up the gasoline stove and soon we feasted on bacon, eggs, and coffee before we resumed the journey west.

U.S. 40 was the road to be traveled. It led through the Ohio towns of Cambridge, Zanesville, Newark and on to the city of Columbus where we arrived on the third day of our journey.

Columbus was a thriving city, and driving through it required several hours. Electrically-operated cars—then called "Street Cars," or trolleys, ran through the city, and the driver of an automobile had to be careful to avoid the car rails as well as the cars.

We pitched our tent west of Columbus in a farmer's field. In 1924, there were no Holiday Inns, Ramada Inns or Town Houses—none of the great motel chains which now cater to automobile traffic. There were a few small buildings called "Tourist camps," some of which had places to pitch a tent, obtain tap water and cook a meal. A few enterprising housewives and farmers placed signs on their houses or in their yards offering "Rooms for Tourists"—usually for one or two dollars per night.

Highway direction signs were rare, and one was frequently required to stop and ask directions, usually at old livery stables which had been converted into garages.

By the seventh day we found ourselves somewhere in Indiana and very short of money. I had been designated as "Business Manager" and began to solicit business in sign painting. Because of our youth, we usually had difficulty getting our first job. However, after Tater painted the first sign, his excellent work was available for showing, and we had no difficulty in getting further jobs so that soon our finances were in excellent shape and we could continue on our travels West.

My friend Bill had always wanted to be a cowboy and, at his

request, we decided to travel through the Northwest. Before we started, we had equipped our car with what we thought were excellent tires, but we soon began to have many flats. On just one day, while touring in the Dakotas, we had thirteen flats and our gasoline tank dropped off. We wired it on with some barbed wire "borrowed" from a farmer's fence, patched our leaky inner tubes, and continued on our way.

From Des Moines, Iowa, we were directed by a member of the Chamber of Commerce with an apparent interest in the gasoline stations on the highway, to take the Yellowstone Trail.

It was Bill and his desire to see more "cowboy country" that led us through such towns as "Fish Creek" and "Deadwood" in South Dakota, and to visit the graves of Wild Bill Hickok and Calamity Jane.

The Dakotas in those days were great horse country but not so great for cars. From Des Moines, Iowa, west to the state of Washington, there were no hard roads. The roads that existed were gravel and so narrow that passing usually required one or the other automobile to back up to a "turning-out place," depending on who won the argument.

We followed the Yellowstone Trail through the Badlands of South Dakota. For a West Virginia "Ridge Runner" this was strange country, indeed. It was a dry, desert land with endless, odd stone formations and there, camping one dark, moonless night, I heard, for the first time in my life, the howl of a wild coyote.

We left that land, once the hiding place of Outlaw Bands, and set out across the dry and desolate, sparsely-settled state of Wyoming. We drove until we reached the higher areas around Yellowstone Park. Entering the park through the Cody Gate, we were awed and astounded by the beauty and vastness of the place. It contained thirty-five hundred acres. We spent five days touring Yellowstone Park, pitching our tent each night in the area provided for tent campers. There were numerous wild animals in the park, including bears which would come up to the car hoping to be fed. Feeding the bears, then as now, was forbidden because, though appearing tame, they would sometimes bite or maul unsuspecting tourists.

127

From Yellowstone we journeyed through Idaho and into Washington State, arriving in Spokane, broke from our trip to Yellowstone. Hungry, and in need of funds to continue our trip, we decided to fall back on our painting skills. We lived for six weeks in a tourist camp and saved enough money to continue our tour of Seattle, Washington, then through Oregon and on to Oakland, California.

We were unable to find work in California; so we started home, across the Great Desert from Bakersfield, California, to Needles and on to Phoenix, Arizona.

The roads were sand and gravel; the heat was a searing 125 to 130 degrees. We passed through one 90-mile stretch of desert which had not one single human habitation. The trip from California to Arizona took four days in which we were plagued by recurring flat tires and much overheating of our car.

Along the desert road we found the scattered bones of dead cattle and horses and the remains of broken wagons, a silent testament to the hardships experienced by the early settlers on their "Westward Journey" many years before.

Westward, Forty-six Years Later

My good wife Rebecca and I left Morgantown early one November morning to retrace parts of my earlier journey West. Much of the route was the same, or close to the same that Tater, Bill and I had traveled. The differences were interesting to note.

My 1924 four-cylinder Chevy had been replaced by a 1969 eight-cylinder Dodge Sedan, the speed of which was limited only by the sanity of the driver; instead of chugging along at 40, we could cruise comfortably at 60.

Unlike our Chevy tires which seemed to go flat every half-hour, the tires on our Dodge gave us not one single flat all the way from Morgantown, West Virginia, to Phoenix, Arizona, a distance of nearly twenty-five hundred miles.

Some of the new road followed the path formed earlier by the National Pike. Gone were the bumpy, gravel roads, re-

128

placed by smooth, fine highways, by-passing the towns along the way. I wondered if the time we saved was worth the sights of the cities we had missed. From Wheeling, into Ohio, through Cambridge and Zanesville, past the statue of Barbara Zane in the town square, through Newark, we were in Columbus by 12:30 p.m. of the same day we began. Although not impressive by today's standards, in retrospect to 1924, it was quite a feat.

We glimpsed from a distance towns we had earlier driven through and, arriving at Terre Haute, Indiana, almost six hundred miles of our journey behind us, we stopped for the night.

There was no tent to pitch along the highway this time. Instead, we found a handy Holiday Inn. Admittedly, it was not as cheap, but, considering we had steak dinner instead of canned beans and slept under clean, white sheets instead of rolled-in blankets, it was well worth the cost.

On the second day of our trip we passed through Lincoln country, and I wondered what he, once a young circuit-riding lawyer, would have thought of the "progress" and the speed by which one now made passage on the journey west.

We crossed the Mississippi at Saint Louis and were "allowed" to view some of the city as the by-pass had not yet been completed. This, the highway signs informed us, was "Jesse James Country." At the end of the day we were "waylaid" by another Holiday Inn sign and bedded down too weary to worry about bank robbers.

Passing the friendly Indian at the toll booth, we continued on across the picturesque landscape of Oklahoma through Tulsa and, following the Will Rogers Highway, on to Amarillo, Texas.

Riding over the wide, limited access highways, I was reminded by the contrast of the narrow, gravel roads of my earlier trip. Some change!

On through the Cimarron country, known also as the Cherokee Nation, we traveled.

We passed through oceans of buffalo grass. Where once the buffalo grazed, we saw only fine, fat Hereford cattle. On roadsigns we read names like Broken Arrow, Cherokee, and Fairland.

Leaving the Will Rogers Highway behind, we drove "over"

Oklahoma City and on to Amarillo. El Reno, Elk City, Shamrock and McLean were some of the towns we passed through in this fine farm country of the Texas panhandle. There were fields of grain, grain elevators, steaks on the hoof and a place to rest in Amarillo. Juice, coffee, eggs, and "Texas fried" potatoes awaited us in the morning before we began our journey on to Tucumcari, New Mexico.

New Mexico, Land of Enchantment! It is almost a "moonscape." Nothing must have changed here in millions of years; nothing, perhaps, but the roads and the cars and the faces of the travelers.

We followed the road to Santa Fe, the home of an old friend, spending the night in an old, pueblo style hotel known as The La Fonda.

Santa Fe could easily be called one of the most unique cities in America. It is built mostly in the simple but elegant style of architecture of the Pueblo Indian dwellings.

From Santa Fe we traveled south to Albuquerque, New Mexico, the home of the Navajos. From New Mexico we traveled to Flagstaff, Arizona, over a high plateau of the Rocky Mountains, dangerous in the winter, but on this autumn day we saw only a few traces of snow. We saw snow from a distance at Flagstaff, on the top of Humphrey Peak.

Our temptation to head north to the Grand Canyon was tempered by the very real possibility of being snowed in, and so we headed south instead. We followed Highway 17 on a hundred-mile downgrade into the Valley of The Sun, and there, at Scottsdale, our second Westward Journey was done.

A Conversational Postscript

During the five days of traveling across this beautiful land, we encountered many friendly, kind people; however, as usual in the smaller mountain towns, one occasionally encounters the hungry individual, usually at a gas station, who tries to frighten him into buying new tires, fan belts or shock absorbers.

In Holbrook, Arizona, I stopped for gasoline, and after the

tank had been filled while my wife was visiting the rest room the following conversation took place between myself and the attendant.

The attendant: "You owe me five dollars and a quarter."
Me: "O.K., here's my Standard Oil Card."
The attendant: "Your left shock absorber is worn out. It is dangerous to drive that way. I can replace it."
Me: "No, I like it that way—I drive that way all the time."
The attendant: "You will lose $40.00 worth of your front tire. If you knew anything about it you would change it."
Me: "No, I'm just an old hillbilly from West Virginia and I like it that way."

He continued to argue that I should buy a new shock absorber. I finally said, "Now, I have traveled these roads for a number of years, and there is always someone trying to frighten me into buying something." He replied, "If you wasn't such a dumb son-of-a-bitch you would know what I was talking about."

I replied that I didn't think it was a very nice way for an attendant at a Standard Oil Station to talk to a customer.

Otherwise, the journey westward was very enjoyable—and I had no trouble with shock absorbers.

Portrait of a Mountain Woman

She was born in a little village called Albrightsville—a small town with a post office and one store. The town was snuggled between two mountains. Cheat River ran between the mountains. It was a fast-moving stream coming from higher mountains through valleys, a few miles to the north.

People lived on both sides of the river—a bridge crossed it. There was no railroad when she was born.

The date of her birth was February 12, 1858. She was the daughter of a romance between Jacob Welch and Rebecca Martin. Theirs was a Civil War romance commenced shortly before the Fourth of July, 1863, when her husband-to-be met with

131

many other young men near the Baptist Church in the village and enlisted for three years to defend their country in the war.

Upon his return from many battles, from the Mountains of Romney, Virginia, to the plains of the Appomattox, they were married. A year later a daughter was born—they named her Winnie Tree Welch.

There were no free schools until 1863 in what was to become West Virginia. However, by the time she was five years old, small schoolhouses had been built and she commenced her learning—reading, writing and arithmetic being the main subjects taught in the little schoolhouses. She was a brilliant student, studying hard and completing the county school system at the age of fifteen.

There was no high school in her mountain village, but there was a school called an academy some seven miles away in a village called Terra Alta, named because it was on a mountain top. There she enrolled, and for three or more years pursued what was then known as a higher education.

Also, pursuing their education there was a man who was to become famous in West Virginia, Frank Butler Trotter and his brother. Frank was to become president of West Virginia University, and his brother, Russell, a teacher of law there. Many others in this school were to become judges and high public officials.

Having completed the education then available in that mountain region at the age of nineteen years, she was offered a position as a schoolteacher.

She taught for thirteen years in various mountain schools, riding a horse or mule to get to the schoolhouse, boarding and rooming at the nearest good homes. Her salary was never more than forty dollars a month, and the term of school was, in those days, five months.

During the summer months when there was no school, she attended the academy or worked in her father's post office, where he had been appointed postmaster by President Grant, his old commanding officer when he was a Sergeant under the General in the Army of the Potomac.

She was a very attractive woman. When I grew to manhood,

many men whom she taught often told me about how much they admired her beauty and her ability to teach them.

One day a young man came into the post office to mail a letter, and as she was working that day they met and a romance developed. In a few months she became the wife of Raymond Walter Mason.

They moved to Morgantown where their first child, Medora Mason, was born in 1900. Her parents were growing old, Albright was becoming a booming lumber village, and a railroad had been built; so they returned to Albright, the town having changed its name from Albrightsville. There they started a hotel and small store built adjacent to the old homestead.

Their second child, a son, was born January 18, 1903, and they named him Kermit Raymond Mason. Another daughter was born in 1905 and was named Genevive Winifred Mason.

Now, their family was complete, and their education was commenced—first, in the home, since having been a schoolteacher, she read to them in the evenings around a large Burnside stove. The books she read were the classics. *Ben Hur* was the one I remember the most, but there were also English and French novels. She taught us children not only to read, but also to have a love of good literature before we even entered the first grade in school.

You who were born in country towns in the early 1900s will recall that they were without sewers, there were no water lines and no running water, nor were there water heaters in many homes. Bathtubs were only seen in your mail-order catalogs. So, Saturday night, especially in the winter months, great pots of water were heated on the kitchen coal burning stoves. A large bathtub was brought into the living room near the old Burnside stove, and each of us children was scrubbed clean and sent to bed. The next morning being Sunday, we put on our best clothes, shined our shoes, and were taken to Sunday School in the little white "M.E." (Methodist Episcopal) church situated on the banks of Cheat River.

There we learned our lessons about the Bible stories and the rules of a good life as set forth in the Ten Commandments. Too, as we grew older we stayed to hear long sermons by eloquent preachers. Then, as we matured, there was Epworth League

133

where each of us must lead when our turn came, as leadership was rotated among those attending.

Sunday dinners were usually large affairs. Often, neighbors dined with us and also many times the preacher, who existed on a small salary, and depended partly upon donations given to him by his flock.

Grandmother Welch occupied a part of the house, and as she was a very devout Christian woman, she attended prayer meetings on Wednesday nights. Frequently I accompanied her to the church carrying a kerosene lantern since there were no street lights in the village.

The ladies of the Methodist congregation, which consisted of people who traveled in their wagons, buggies and on horseback for miles around in the mountain and valleys where most of them lived on farms, each month put on a chicken and waffle dinner. These were great affairs and had for their purpose the raising of money to keep the church's financial affairs in order. My mother was a good cook and assisted in preparing these dinners which were a very enjoyable part of the social life of her mountain community.

I'll always remember the enjoyable taste of a meal of good fried chicken dumplings and brown waffles with gravy, that was usually topped off with a large dish of ice cream and apple pie prepared and served by these fine ladies of the Methodist church.

There was no crime in our little community; none of the people even locked their doors.

If someone was sick and needed aid, the word soon spread, and every neighbor was willing to aid and did come to their aid. There was no government relief in those days; and I'm sure if there had been, these mountain people would have been too proud to accept it.

When someone died, neighbors came to the home and expressed their sympathy by bringing large quantities of food. Also it seemed that everyone in the village and for miles around attended the deceased's funeral, thus, showing their respect.

School also played a large part in our lives and those of everyone in the community. Plays were put on, debates were held, and the whole community seemed to attend and take part.

My mother bought one of the first pianos that I remember seeing in our village. Many evenings the young people would gather in our home. My sister, Medora, would play the popular songs, such as the old hymns; and all would join in the singing. Thus, our home became a popular place for many of the youths, and frequent happy evenings were spent.

During World War I, 1917-1918, our community was very prosperous due to war needs, with lumber and coal being produced in great quantities; and then when the war demands ended, there was little demand for these commodities. Many people were out of work. My father's and mother's business, like all others in the community, began to decline, and what the mountain people called "hard times" set in.

Mother seemed worried. When she had an opportunity to purchase a small farm on a hillside about two miles from Albright, she and dad bought the property, and we moved there. The little farm consisted of less than ten acres. It had a good two-bedroom house. There was a fine spring of water, and for the first time we had water piped into the kitchen. There was a barn, a chicken house, a hog pen, and the usual "back house" or, in more refined terms, a privy. We added two rooms to the house for sleeping. A large basement contained a good coal furnace and a large place to store vegetables.

Mother, from her experience in teaching school and living in farm homes, had some experience in farm life. Dad had none but was willing to learn.

A cow was purchased—a good Jersey that gave rich milk from which delicious tasty butter was made. Pigs were purchased along with chickens. The move was in the spring. A neighboring farmer plowed a few acres for us. Corn, potatoes, and beans were planted.

Fall came, and we had a beautiful harvest. Mother canned the corn. We children picked the beans, many of which were canned, while others were placed in the large basement to dry and be eaten later. Many bushels of potatoes were dug and placed in the basement.

Our chickens were supplying us with a surplus of eggs, and some of them were sold at the Albright store. Berries were

135

picked, and mother made delicious jams. The pigs were butchered, and the meat cured for the winter months.

We now had plenty to eat during the coming winter. A few loads of coal were hauled by a neighboring farmer, and the furnace kept us warm all winter.

I arose early before schooltime and milked the cow, fed the chickens and pigs, and was off to school. Father sold nursery stock and paint. This required him to travel to adjacent towns where he would spend a few days. He liked his home, and when he thought he had earned enough for our needs, he would return.

We children were in high school during our farm period, but the Albright High School was closed because of the scarcity of students. During those years most young men were not interested in "more schooling," as they called it then, after the eighth grade.

For a period of two years we were bused to school in Kingwood. Upon our return home, mother would have delicious meals prepared—ham, hot soup, a kettle of which was almost always on the stove, home baked white bread, corn bread ("corn pone" we called it), and delicious pies made from pumpkins or apples gathered on our small farm.

There were no radios or televisions and few amusements. We had plenty of time to study our lessons in the evenings, and mother saw to it that we did. If we were poor, we did not know it.

There were good, happy years. Time passed fast, and in 1918 Medora finished high school and secured a job as a teacher in a county school. In 1921 I was graduated from Kingwood High School—Genevive was a junior.

Now, a new era was about to commence. Should we children go to college? Father, among his other activities, had been a painter of houses and bridges. He was sure I could make a good living at it. Mother was determined that I would have a college education.

At this time father was sixty-three years old; mother was fifty-three. Father was contented with his home, but mother, being the dominant one in the family, decided we would move to Morgantown, West Virginia, where her children could go to the State University. There was much argument between the two, but in the end mother prevailed. To Morgantown we would move.

Upon a day in June 1921, we, with me as the driver, mother and dad and I set off in the family car for Morgantown. Upon arriving there, dad visited the real estate office of a John W. Wiles, the leading realtor. Mother wanted a large house close to the university where she hoped to run a rooming and boarding house for university students. Neither had much money, but finally a home was selected and finances arranged.

We returned home to Albright, sold our mountain house, our livestock, and most of our furniture and moved into our new home on Union Street—now Dallas Street in Morgantown. How they had the courage to do this at their advanced ages, I will never know.

Soon dad secured a contract to paint sixty or more of the "company" houses owned by the Bethlehem Steel Company in Richard, West Virginia, and a contract to paint a bridge in Cadell, upriver from Albright. I took charge of the bridge job, and dad started the Richard one. A number of our Albright friends were employed on both jobs. Mother cooked for the employees and they boarded in our home when painting houses in Richard.

I entered the university in the fall of 1921, and Medora a year later. Mother arose at dawn and cooked huge meals for some eight or nine university students. She worked long hours into the evenings. Several of the students roomed in our house, but the pay was very small. Mother and dad moved into the attic of the house. The basement was improved and rented.

After the first year I was determined to quit school and go to work as a painter. Long, determined arguments as to the value of a college education were made by mother. She was determined that I would not disappoint her. Seeing the hardships she was going through, I secured work on Saturdays and holidays and earned some small amounts of money.

Dad started a secondhand clothing store as the years of the late twenties were "depression years." He did very well, and after about four years mother gave up the idea of trying to cook for and feed hungry students. She did, however, rent a few rooms. Genevive got a job teaching a rural school and helped with the family chores.

These were hard years for mother and dad. How they made it, I will never know. Mother had great determination, patience, perseverance and great love for her children—and she and dad prevailed; for in 1927 Kermit received a degree in law, Medora a degree in journalism, and Genevive married a young engineer. They were a proud mother and father who watched their son and daughter and their son-in-law don their black robes and march to the fieldhouse of West Virginia University where they received their diplomas.

I shall always remember the look of happiness on their faces as this event occurred.

Never did a mother show such love for her children—nor did any father and mother sacrifice more than they did to see that their children secured college educations. Mother would say, "An education is something no one can steal or take away from you." The years passed—Genevive moved to Charleston where her husband had a good job with Union Carbide. Medora became the head of the Journalism Department in Fairmont State Normal School. Kermit was employed by the U.S. Government in Pittsburgh for a year, and then returned to Morgantown to practice law.

Kermit married his lovely girl that he met in a chemistry class. They bought a home on Madigan Avenue.

Dad was now seventy-two and mother sixty-two. They lost their mortgaged home on Dallas Street, and I helped them build a little home near our residence on Madigan Avenue. Dad never got to live in it—only to have his funeral there because he died from an operation in 1932. Mother, however, moved into the house, and when our children came along, four in five years, was very happy with them; and they loved her dearly.

I continued to practice law in Morgantown and Medora taught in Fairmont Normal. It was a great pleasure for me to furnish mother with all her needs, and Medora helped too. I think they were happy years for her.

And then World War II commenced in 1941. I had practiced law for almost fifteen years, but having been instilled with patriotism and love of country by my mother, I secured a commission and entered the armed forces in 1942. When I left for overseas' duty, she did not cry, but smiled and said, "If I were forty years younger, I would go with you."

From Africa and Italy, I wrote her and she wrote me many letters. I still have and treasure them.

On a day in the spring of 1944 at the age of 76, she peacefully passed away. I received a telegram eight days later telling me of her death. No woman ever lived with more courage and love for her family. She was a truly outstanding mountain woman!

Mother and Her 'Pinkum' Dress

My mother, during her early years, was a schoolteacher. She had attended the Terra Alta Academy for teachers and possessed a very good education for those early years of our country before the early 1900s.

The rural schools in those days were in the sparsely populated areas of the West Virginia hills. There were no school buses. The children walked to school, often for a distance of several miles. All grades convened in a single one-room building heated by a wood or coal burning stove in the middle of the room. One teacher was in charge, and in addition to teaching administered discipline to the pupils who were made up of the very young to the almost adult.

Mother was a very proud woman and was very careful of her dress. One particular morning she was wearing a pink silk dress.

Mary Moats was about seventeen years old. She was a troublemaker in the Welch School. She often made faces and kept the younger children in an uproar. Mother had talked to her many times, trying to maintain order in her country school.

On this day, Mary seemed worse than usual, causing much disturbance in the school; and finally mother told her she must leave the room and return home for the day.

Mary arose in a dignified manner, raised her arms and almost screamed, "Farewell, farewell, farewell, Welch School, farewell forever!" Then pointing her hand at my mother, the teacher, she yelled, "I hope to God you shit your pinkum dress!" She slammed the door as she left and never returned.

Mother said she never wore that dress to her school again!

139

Unfamiliar Language

John Harrington Cox was a very polished gentleman of the old school tradition. He was an English professor at West Virginia University. He had traveled widely and had studied English Literature at Oxford University in England.

At the time of this story he was then engaged in collecting old folklore tales from the backwoods counties of West Virginia where the early English pioneers had settled.

He arrived at a mountain cabin far back in the hills of Mingo County, West Virginia, one evening near sundown and asked if he could stay the night. After being questioned as to whether or not he was a "revenueman," and after he had accepted a drink of moonshine liquor from the jug, he was escorted to a lean-to attached to the cabin, where he spent the night. He was awakened at daylight the next morning and escorted to the cabin for breakfast.

Seven growing sons were seated with their father at a round hand-carved table. Five growing girls and their mother were cooking large pancakes which were being consumed by all the males at the table almost as fast as they were supplied by the women.

Professor Cox was given some cakes, and although he several times said, "Please pass the gravy," no one responded. The boys would look at him in wonder each time he said, "Please pass the gravy," and then at their father. Finally, after six or seven times unsuccessful tries to get the gravy for his cakes, he was rescued from the impasse. One of the older sons looked at his father and said, "Pap, the damned fool means the Sop!"

Professor Cox was passed the gravy!

George Mason,
the Author of the Bill of Rights
in the U.S. Constitution

Jefferson, Washington, Patrick Henry, John Adams and Thomas Paine are the most talked of and written about during the second hundred years of the founding of our great nation. However, there is one man who, perhaps, had more to do than any other with the making of our Constitution. Until recently his name was scarcely mentioned. That man was George Mason, of Gunston Hall, Virginia.

Among the first revolutionaries, George Mason had drafted the Non-Importation Agreement thus breaking economic ties with England. He drafted the first Declaration of Rights for Virginia and the Virginia Constitution. These documents later became the basic principles of the United States Constitution. The Bill of Rights which was added thirteen years later was almost identical to the Virginia Bill of Rights.

Mason was the fourth George Mason. He was descended from the First George Mason who came to Virginia in 1650 to escape the armies of Oliver Cromwell. He built a plantation. His descendants continued to reside on the land and added thereto.

The fourth George Mason was born in 1725 on the plantation which adjoined Mount Vernon. He was a friend and neighbor of George Washington. Washington and Mason were both in the Virginia House of Burgesses, and while there Mason wrote some of Washington's state papers.

Being a leader in Virginia, George Mason was elected as a delegate to the National Constitutional Convention in Philadelphia. While there, he insisted upon designating a time for the ending of slavery even though at the time he was operating a five-thousand-acre plantation with slaves. Furthermore, he believed the Constitution as prepared was worthless without a Bill of Rights and for these reasons refused to sign the same.

The Bill of Rights, being the first ten amendments to our U.S. Constitution, was proposed by Congress in 1789 and was finally adopted in 1791 in almost the identical wording which Mason had prepared and attempted to get adopted in the Philadelphia Convention.

Without the Bill of Rights which guarantees freedom of the press, freedom of speech, freedom of religious worship, and many other rights, our great nation would not have held together.

George Mason had nine children; six sons and three

daughters who survived him when he died in 1792. He and his brothers left many descendants.

George Mason's will is particularly interesting in this political and bi-centennial year of 1976:

> I recommend it to my sons from my own experience in life, to prefer the happiness of independence and a private station to the troubles and vexation of public business, but if either their own inclination or the necessity of the times should engage them in public affairs, I charge them on a father's blessing, never to let the motives of private interest or ambition induce them to betray, nor the terrors of poverty and disgrace, nor the fear of danger or of death, deter them from asserting the liberty of their country and endeavoring to transmit to their posterity those sacred rights to which themselves were born.

Gunston Hall is the name of the home built by George Mason. It has been restored, and is being operated as a public trust. The home and the spacious boxwood gardens surrounding it are well worth visiting. Although my own family of Masons is probably a descendant of George Mason IV, the exact genealogy has not been traced.

Bum Bum

One of the most remarkable characters I have ever known was my grandmother on my mother's side. Her name was Rebecca Martin Welch. She had married my grandfather shortly after he returned from the Civil War in the early 1860s. They had one daughter, my mother, whose name was Winnie.

I have little remembrance of my grandfather Welch since he died when I was about four years old. However, most of my young life was spent with and around Grandmother Welch.

For many years we lived in the same large frame house. It was located at the junction of the two main highways leading to the railroad station which was the center of almost all life in the village of Albright, West Virginia, before the days of the automobile. From the front window grandmother could observe the passersby. She knew most of them, and they frequently waved to her. She was known to all her friends as "Aunt Beck."

She must have been nearing seventy years old when I was born. My earliest recollection of her was when I frequently spent the night with her in her side of the house. I would be awakened in the morning when she was stirring the fire in her coal-burning stove to heat the room. Next I observed her washing her face— not with soap, but with a wet rag with corn meal. She believed soap ruined one's complexion. She used much of it elsewhere, but never on her face, and she did possess a beautiful face with a fine complexion and very few wrinkles even when she was nearing the age of ninety years.

Next, before I could read, and before breakfast, she would read to me a chapter from her well-worn Bible. After I was older and could read, she required me to read the chapter to her. After reading the Bible, she and I knelt for a moment in prayer, and then we had our breakfast—usually eggs and buckwheat cakes. She baked large thin buckwheat cakes, the batter of which had been set in the early fall and renewed frequently—and whose delicious taste I have not had since, but still remember. Such a cake covered with an egg or sausage was a thrilling delight for a hungry, growing boy. Once in later years when she was quite old she coyly told me she had included Epsom salts in small quantities in the cakes to aid her digestion and that she hoped they agreed with me.

Grandmother Welch, I was told, had been an invalid for sixteen years in her younger days and had not been able to walk. Her friends had subscribed money and sent her to Johns Hopkins Hospital in Baltimore, Maryland. She had recovered completely.

She belonged to the Methodist church and was very devout in her faith. Though her entire income was from grandfather's Civil War pension, she believed in tithing and gave ten percent of it to the church and the missionary society. She attended all the church services—both on Sunday and the Wednesday night prayer meetings. It was my job to accompany her there. She would have her lantern ready and we would walk to the church. There she would sit in the same seat in the second row from the front. She never professed to be more pious than the other person, nor attempted to impose her faith on others who had different opinions.

Nothing seemed to worry her—she was always content and happy. I never heard her complain about anything, including the weather. Nor did I ever hear her talk about or criticize any one in the entire community.

With the exception of her trip to the hospital in Baltimore, she had traveled very little until she decided to go to Iowa by train and visit her relatives. She was nearly eighty then, and my mother was worried about her making the trip alone. However, she did go alone by train and enjoyed the two months she spent in the West.

Each birthday I received a dollar from her with a note complimenting me and with a word of advice. But never did I receive a word of criticism from her.

The people in the village brought their troubles to her and came to her for advice. She was always concerned with the sick and visited them. She knew many home remedies and administered to the ill as there were few doctors in those days.

Our family moved from the village, and she continued to live alone. However, we often visited her and after I was through school and married, she would visit us for a few weeks at a time in the winter months, but always paying something, as she said, for her room and board. Though we had small children, she seemed to enjoy them and nothing seemed to destroy her peace of mind. They, too, seemed to enjoy her and gave her the name of "Bum-Bum," apparently derived from an old folk story she told them. She was a good storyteller and entertained them for many an hour as she had me—when I was their age.

She was past ninety years when one day I received a call from one of her neighbors in the village saying I had better come to see her as she was quite ill. I went immediately. She told me she had lived a long time and had enjoyed life—that she was about to leave this world, that she was not afraid. She instructed me about her burial, and the next day she died. Her funeral was one of the largest ever held in her village. The preacher read the poem, "Let me live in a house by the side of the road and be a friend to man."

She had really been a friend to all.

Why I Am for a Third Medical Opinion

By 1934 we had three young sons—they had arrived a little more than a year apart.

We were anxious to have a daughter. My wife became pregnant, and after a few months she became ill. We called a doctor. After examining my wife, he said, "I think it will endanger your wife's health to have this child." He suggested an abortion.

Our laws then were very strict on abortion, and the doctor suggested that we call in another doctor for a consultation before removing my wife to a local hospital to perform the abortion.

The two doctors consulted long, and then called me in and suggested an immediate abortion. I was very hesitant and so was my wife. I suggested to them we wait a day or two. They did not think this wise, but reluctantly agreed.

Our personal doctor, a large man who loved the outdoors, was on a fishing trip, I located him by phone, and he immediately returned. He carefully examined my wife and then said, "I don't believe an abortion is necessary. Let's put her to bed for a week and prop up her feet. You know you may have a daughter—you've always wanted one—if she is permitted to live. She might be a great comfort to you in your old age."

We consented. In a few months, a lovely baby arrived: Five-and-one-half pounds with blue eyes and golden hair. We named her Rebecca Welch Mason, the Welch being an ancestral name. So the three brothers, Tom, Dick and Bill, age from five years to sixteen months, now had a baby sister.

She was a healthy girl, and as the years went by she grew into a "tom boy," playing all the games boys played. She could bat a baseball, throw a football, ride a pony and a bicycle. We had a camp on a lake. She soon learned to operate a motorboat. She became an ardent fisherwoman.

We took all four children on many vacations to Canada. She could outswim, outrun, and was a better fisherwoman than the boys.

I could write a book about her achievements. No one would probably read it. I write this in hopes that many children like her will be given the right to live, and that unnecessary abortions will be abolished forever.

Rebecca Mason Perry had forty-eight years of happy life thanks to an honest doctor—now, long departed, hoping, however, that she too may know of this in Heaven where she must be.

Thank God her life was not destroyed by an abortion before she became our lovely daughter—wife and mother, and gave us a beautiful, intelligent, sweet, lovely granddaughter, Kimberly Perry, whose life will make her mother now in Heaven proud.

(Written in 1984.)

To My Daughter in Heaven

God gave us a beautiful golden-haired blue-eyed daughter on April 14, 1934. This was one of the happiest days of our lives. We had three lovely, healthy sons, named Tom, Dick, and Bill, all of whom were close together, ranging from two to seven. Our family was now complete—three sons and a daughter.

God was good to us from the day of our marriage in 1927. We had enjoyed prosperity and good health. Now, our lovely family continued to grow and develop into adults.

From the time she was a year old, Becky, as we had named our daughter Rebecca after her mother and grandmother, who was then approaching the age of ninety years, became a playmate with her brothers. She was a healthy girl; she joined in all sports with her brothers including football and baseball. No matter how rough the sports became, Becky was in the thick of the same.

We were a hiking family—often taking long hikes into the mountains near our home in West Virginia. Becky was usually in the lead. No path was too steep for her, nor any huge rock or tree too large or tall for her to climb.

The years rolled by. We built a camp near Cheat River and spent our summers there. There was a pony, and Becky was the best rider of all. Too, she loved to fish. Our local streams then were polluted, so each year for many before World War II, we all loaded up in our car and drove to northern Canada. She usually caught the largest fish and was also the best swimmer in the northern lakes.

The day Pearl Harbor was bombed, she and I together had been hiking in the woods near our camp. When we returned to our car and turned on the radio, the news was carrying the story about the Japs having attacked our country. I said, "Becky, your daddy will soon have to go to war to help defend our country." She was six years old then.

I entered the army in 1942, and I was saddened to leave my family; but I remember Becky and her brothers calling, "Goodby daddy," as I drove away from our Madigan Avenue home in Morgantown, West Virginia.

To help the war effort she and her brothers gathered iron, aluminum, and junk and lugged it to the Court House square. They took part in all war efforts then in force for civilians.

Soon after entering the army, and after receiving my training, I became Judge Advocate at Fort Sam Houston, in San Antonio, Texas. I secured a home on the post and moved my family there.

These were happy days for Becky and her brothers, and for my wife and myself. There was a dog given to them. They named him Private Jones and built a house for him.

Becky enjoyed watching the troops being trained on the army post. Tom was a great collector of any patches which indicated the many divisions of the army.

Within a few months, I was ordered overseas, and Becky and her brothers and mother returned to our home in Morgantown. She wrote me many letters scribbled in her left-hand writing while I was in Africa and Europe. I enjoyed them greatly and still have a few of them.

The war was over, and on one of the happiest days of my life I was again reunited with my four lovely children and beautiful wife.

School days proceeded. Soon, Becky was a beautiful high school graduate. She entered West Virginia securing an A.B. degree in English, and then a Master's degree in English. She was very brilliant, and her professors often remarked to me as to her great ability. She wrote her Master's thesis in poetry, and the

147

head of the English Department told me he was amazed at her ability.

We visited Florida one winter, and she drove the car all the way. She was not large, and I remember a patrolman stopping the car because he did not think she was old enough to drive. She soon convinved him that she was a mature young lady.

I became interested in politics. She was my greatest campaigner—working long hours, day and night for me. She was more disappointed than I was when I was not elected; however, there were many other elections, and she took part in all of them.

Her mother and I took her to the second Eisenhower Convention in San Francisco, and we returned home through Canada. In Banff, she went horseback riding with a Canadian Mounted Policeman.

Time moved on—many, many happy years together. She taught English one year in West Virginia University. Then, in 1954, she and her mother took the grand tour of Europe: Spain, Italy, France and Germany, where she drank beer and sang along with the German students in Heidelberg.

She met a young student in college, and there was a home wedding. She was a beautiful bride. She and her husband, Robert Kyle Perry, drove away in a Volkswagen that her mother and I gave them for a wedding present. He taught for a year in Point Pleasant High School, and Becky worked in a library close by.

Robert, being a geologist, secured a job with the U.S. Government in the Navy's Oceanographer's Department. They moved to the Washington area in Oxon Hill, Maryland, where they bought a beautiful home. Then a little blue-eyed image of her mother was born. They named her Kimberly ("Kim") Perry. No more children came, and they adopted a boy and named him Scott Perry.

They bought a camp on the beautiful Shenandoah where they spent many happy hours. Once when Kim was just a baby, Becky brought her to visit us when we lived in Carefree, Arizona. Becky and I arose early many mornings, driving into the hills to see the beautiful sunrises.

Robert's work required much ocean travel, and Becky used

148

her spare time touring the many interesting places in Washington. Her home became the visiting places for Tom's children, and Becky gave them many tours of Washington.

Being interested in politics, she visited the White House many times; and on one occasion sat in the President's Box in the Kennedy Center during the Ford Campaign.

Kimberly, her daughter, and her mother were very close. She taught Kim in the ways of the world. Both had the utmost confidence in each other, and complete trust existed between them. Scott loved her, as she gave him all the love and attention a natural mother could give a son. This family of Perrys camped together—played together—swam in the community pool. They lived in a small neighborhood in Oxon Hill and had many friendly neighbors who worked and played together and were enjoying life to its fullest.

Kimberly grew into a talented young lady, having completed her education in a Maryland high school. She entered West Virginia University in 1981, and is now a second-year student there—age nineteen years. Scott is going to the grade school in Oxon Hill, Maryland.

Many trips were made by Becky and her family to our home in Morgantown through the years and her mother and I visited them often in their home. They were to spend Christmas with us in Morgantown in December 1982, before traveling on to California.

A few days before their planned arrival, Becky phoned us saying she was ill and could not come. The next day she was taken to a local hospital, and died within a few days.

Her daughter, Kim, her brother Dick, and her husband were present; and although she had all the medical attention available, she left this world.

My grief as her father will never end. I loved her so. I always thought she should have lived much longer than I would, who am now past eighty years; that she would continue to write beautiful poetry, and be interested in her hobby of collecting antiques—that some day she would see her daughter and son, both of whom she loved, graduated from college and launched upon a happy life-style as she had been.

Her daughter, Kim, and son, Scott, having had a wonderful,

honest, loving mother, must continue their education and take part in life's society as decent, respectable citizens because I'm sure that somewhere out in the great beyond, Becky will be watching and hoping that the dreams she had for them did not die within her body—that her soul survives.

Love never dies.

We had you with us on earth for forty-eight lovely years, and God willing, we will see you in eternity.

Your father,
Kermit R. Mason
Phoenix, Arizona, February 9, 1983

My Granddaughter Kim's Opinion of Me

Of any individual I know, there is only one who can manage to be both the dearest thing to my heart as well as the most exasperating, aggravating, and temper-provoking old man to grace the world, all at the same time! Rightfully so, I am the most temperamental, rebellious, and outspoken of his grandchildren, as we are two of a kind.

Kermit R. Mason: "Grandpa" during family gatherings and periods of congeniality; "KERMIT!" during times of anger, duress and/or vexation. The product of the West Virginia depression, his mother a schoolteacher become boardinghouse matron, she moved the whole family from the back hills of Albright to Morgantown. It was rumored that his father did not take kindly to the notion of moving, though even after a campaign of reasoning and arguing was launched and his attempted escape from the traveling vehicle was made, he eventually accompanied the family. This tale all the more strengthens the family's belief that stubbornness is decidedly hereditary!

K. Mason attended the University of Arizona and West Virginia University where he obtained his law degree. He has endured the hellish nightmare of WW II, has practiced law for some fifty odd years, and has run for various political offices on the Republican ticket. In the late years of his life he has now resigned himself, if not with a little disgruntlement, to spending his days at his lovely home in South Hills, Morgantown, furiously offering advice to any and all who visit, sometimes contrary to their desires to listen.

The primary bone of contention between the two of us lies within those issues of knowledge and experience. Like most elder "authorities," he believes that because he has reached the age of eighty, he now knows everything. I, too, believe this of myself, although I have only reached the elevated age of nineteen. He feels that for others to make mistakes is wasteful and avoidable when he has the right answers for everyone. I feel that making mistakes is the only way one learns. In these respects we are both right and wrong.

Such differences of opinion generally air themselves once or twice a month, causing the sparks to fly in all directions. I have learned to concede the victories to him as he has had the benefit of experience which I lack. Some of those experiences he has shared in this book, and yet, one can only imagine their significance or meaning.

I've watched him finger those scrolled, black hinges taken from the doorway of Adolph Hitler's household; seen the pained light which flickers forth from his eyes when no one is looking. Many of these stories the family has endured until it has become something of a game to see who can escape the room before he launches into another adventure or picks up his book of poetry.

I wonder what motivates him to speak? perhaps it is the noise of the guns.

As I sit back, having finally reached the completion of this manuscript, and reflect upon my own personal experiences with this man I have come to find a greater knowledge of honesty and truth, of strength and weakness, of who I am and who my grandfather really is. I see a man who has tried his best to be just, though sometimes his method of going about it seems mulish and hardheaded to some of us. I see a man who is respected and admired by friends and community alike. I also see a kind and gentle man, sometimes frightened and lonely; a man who witnesses the friends around him slipping away.

I wonder if perhaps that note of desperation in his voice

151

when he talks and reads and commands to be heard, stems from the anguish of a man approaching a time when he can no longer do those things anymore. There are periods of tension in which the family will rebuke him for not seeming to appreciate all that he has—his family, including six great-grandchildren, good health, and prosperity.

But I think that when he talks, he is only trying to make *us* recognize those injustices one finds in a civilization, hoping we will become individuals who will attempt to combat them as he did. I see all this and much, much more as I secretly study his face during a quiet lapse. I hope he feels he has achieved that goal of instilling insight and aggression into his family, at least in me. For if I become half the person that he has become, "the friend to man," then I will consider myself to be truly fortunate.

Kimberly Perry,
Granddaughter

(Written for a freshman English class at West Virginia University in 1981.)